I AM HOME
WITHIN MYSELF

I AM HOME
WITHIN MYSELF

By

Kadine Christie

HAPPY LIFE MEDIA
Fairhope, Alabama, United States

ACKNOWLEDGEMENT

Giving birth to this book, a labor of love, was made possible with the contributions of so many.

To everyone in this book who ignited the passion in me to pen these stories, thanks for inspiring me.

Sharonia McDonald - thank you for calling me from Germany and editing with me while your toddler napped. Dr. Louie Andrews, your detailed comments and resources were my private classroom. Barbara Johnson, every time you read a piece and invited me over for coffee, wine and unending hours of conversation, you brought my stories to life. I think I owe you a red-ink pen. Jasmine Hodges, thanks for accepting the challenge of being my content editor. Judy Robb, we created Magic. You are officially the "Space Queen." Thanks for coming to my home, and reading my entire manuscript out loud. When my body failed, you sat at my bedside. For the laughter and the tears - I am beyond grateful.

To my family, thanks for being my cheerleaders. Mommy, thanks for the stories and for being my family historian. Monalisa, thanks for being my sacred place. Viando, thanks for bringing the world to me. My three darling dears, Zuri, Zahara, and Markolee - thanks for inspiring and encouraging me. My childhood sweetheart, my dear husband Ontonio Christie, thanks for thinking my first draft was amazing.

CONTENTS

FOREWORD

Life is a gift. But the principle running through all life is that it is not simple. It is complex. It is permeated with both good and evil, not always so easily separated. We can see this as a dirty trick played on all of humanity by a deity that allowed a world not more clear cut. Or we can see it simply as the condition necessary for humans to have free will. Whichever way we choose, or some other entirely, the TRICK is dealing with the dilemma, negotiating the messy. How do we live in the face of life that is so blurred? How do we become whole in living when everything seems so split? I've tried. I've watched those around me try. This is some of what I've concluded about the messy task of life in general, my own life in particular.

Chapter One

INHALE.
EXHALE.
BREATHE.

"The curtains in disrepair separated them, their fear of childbirth connect-ed them."

I was born into a kickass love story on the picturesque yet impoverished little island of Jamaica. The year before my birth, the sun's light was not the only source of heat sneaking beneath clothing. On opposite ends of my beautiful island, the mystery of attraction was burgeoning heat of the erotic kind in the lives of two young couples: a farmworker, Vivian, and his lover, Lorna; and a pastor, Jeral, and his wife, Lurline. They were young and in love — their bodies unexplored terrains. It would be months before moments shared between new lovers would manifest into abdomens stretching with new life. And months before two women, strangers at best, met at the nexus of Spalding Hospital, each of them inhaling and exhaling through contractions that would create a lifetime bond.

It was April, the spring of 1981, when the women met at Spalding Hospital. It was the only one of its kind where expectant mothers could deliver new life. Spalding Hospital was a true juxtaposition of dilapidation and progress. It boasted no modern amenities. No meals were served on sanitized trays at breakfast, lunch, or dinner. A hot meal was not to be had at this hospital; patients had to bring thermoses to keep their food hot. Expecting mothers had to also bring along their own toiletry kits: gowns, bed sheets, and even white-cloth nappies for newborn bums.

There were no locally trained doctors. Cuba, two hundred thirty-seven air miles away, was the closest country that provided training for those wishing to take the Hippocratic oath. These doctors were assisted by self-appointed Jamaican nurses with surgeon-like egos who governed the maternity ward with iron fists. The few nurses moved briskly between the ragged, sheer curtains that separated a line of screeching spring mattresses. Privacy was a vague illusion. Though the hospital was inadequately administered, it represented progress to young Jamaican women of 1981, who all had been born at home. These young women were the first generation afforded the option of giving birth in a hospital setting. Lorna and Lurline were among them.

Outside, Jamaica's physical beauty prospered. Despite its grandeur, the fascinating depth of its gullies and soaring heights of its mountains, many people were still living in the valley of misguided misogynistic ideologies. While some successfully straddled the transformations of the present and the traditions of the past, most still believed that men should not be present during the labor and delivery of their children. Young women were left totally alone in the task of giving birth. They whimpered at the thought, their throats tied in knots with unshed tears.

The strangers Lorna and Lurline lay nervously in their beds across from each other. While the curtains in disrepair separated them, their fear of childbirth connected them. It was their common circumstance — the carrying of life within them — that would grant them the first few moments of introductory dialogue. However, it was humanity's innate need to connect and the long journey of motherhood ahead that catapulted them into a budding relationship that would forever change and merge their lives.

Lorna's body was the first summoned into labor. It started with what felt like a piercing, then increased in intensity with the passing of time. The invisible pain pelted her petite body, eliciting muffled moans that gradually escalated into groans and unintelligible words. The ward was somnolent, and while others stirred with little urgency or care, Lurline awoke to Lorna's growing moans. Lurline was overdue and should have been the one in labor. She shifted her stalwart body on her bed, maneuvered her swollen and wobbly feet one before the other, held the bottom of her protruding abdomen, and waddled to Lorna's bedside. Lurline was a religious woman, married to a pastor, with the two of them leading a small church in their community up in the Cascade Mountains. She was the praying kind, so she prayed without thought or concern for her impassioned tone. Seeing her new friend in such agony was akin to watching a body being split in two. It was almost as if her new friend was possessed by another being. Lurline was witnessing childbirth for the first time and it truly terrified her. She prayed for her new friend and for the pain that she herself would soon endure. Lurline held Lorna's hand through each contraction and breathed with her in unison.

Lorna grew up in a time when certain subjects were not discussed — childbirth being one of them — so she was not mentally or physically prepared. The nurses had a draconian way of handling the ward, and they did not take pity on first-time mothers. Lorna was not exempt.

Unbeknownst to the nurses, Lorna's body was in grave danger. She was hemorrhaging. As a result, she became lethargic. Her legs shook involuntarily. The brown of her irises receded to pure white, and her mind ebbed and flowed between awareness and oblivion. Her body lay still, and the nurses — finally aware of the danger Lorna had been experiencing — busied themselves around her. She was surrounded by complete darkness.

It would be hours before she was able to hear her baby's cry. On Monday, April 13th, Lorna awoke to the sight of the most beautiful blessing she had ever received. She was finally able to hold the child she had nurtured and carried within her for the past nine months. When she regained consciousness, it was decided she needed to remain an extra four nights for observation. Lorna's happiness knew no bounds; the presence of her daughter was enough to eliminate the fear that was imminent during childbirth. Felicity had replaced fear.

Lurline had still not delivered her child, and the weight was starting to physically and mentally drain her. She had thought she was prepared to deliver her own baby, but after seeing Lorna's body contort with pain and hearing the cacophony of screams, Lurline became filled with fright. She was consumed with worry. She cringed at the thought of pushing life from her own body and became overwhelmed with anxiety. It perplexed her that the space that once gave her such pleasure would now be a source of intense pain.

She was not prepared when the doctor came in with some unexpected news: her baby was breech! A risky Cesarean surgery, which was relatively new in Jamaica, was her only option. Lurline had never thought about this, but the doctor told her that her life and the baby's were in danger. She might even have to choose between them. The words your life or your baby's terrorized her. She couldn't believe she had heard the doctor correctly. How could they expect her to choose her life over the child growing within her? Words spoken came to life, and she contemplated the vastness of what she had been asked to decide. Life or death? Hers or her unborn's? Whom should she save? Lurline struggled with one of the predictable truisms of life: always, without cease, being tossed between extremes.

Lurline sat within the confines of her thoughts. The doctor's clear declaration clawed through her mind. The fresh memories of the tumultuous yet tender days of her marriage, the creation of life blossoming within her, and finally the moment when she would hold the physical expression of shared passion. Her thoughts swayed back and forth like a pendulum, tossing her between thoughts of life and death. Lurline turned to her only source of solace. She clasped her hands and prayed. Her inner turmoil found an inkling of light and she made the decision: the baby's life had to be saved.

Lurline suffered alone with the gravity of this decision. Despite her husband's absence during the birthing process, they managed life together. They had started building a home for the family they were creating. They maintained a farm and also a church. Jeral had made the long and treacherous journey to the hospital when it was time for his wife to deliver their child. However, he was not allowed to stay so he had returned home. He was unaware of the turmoil Lurline was facing in his absence. Lurline lay in the hospital bed, thinking about how her husband was going to react when he came to take his family home, but would only be given his child. She saw his face, perplexed by the doctor's words and imagined how forlorn he would become. She visualized his hands,

full with life, reaching out to denounce but instead con-
firming that she was, in fact, absent from her body. He
would come to know two opposing enigmas: the wonder
and warmth of new life and the clammy, cold feel of a
lifeless body.

Lurline inhaled what was her life: her church, her
husband, and her growing belly. Then she exhaled for
what could have been: their long marriage, raising their
baby, and their rightful future. She held her Bible in her
right hand and traced the shining letters on the front —
The Holy Bible. She placed her left hand on the Bible,
and the sight of her ring glittering in light from the window caused dormant memories of her wedding day to
come alive. She had not removed the ring since Jeral had
placed it on her finger. She attempted to remove it now,
but each twirl robbed her of breath, almost as if the ring
encircled her throat. She whimpered at the sight of her
Bible and her wedding ring. In life they were her identity,
but in death they would become her memory.

Lurline needed to confide in someone. She needed her husband to know what had happened in her last moments. As she approached Lorna, holding her Bible and wedding ring, she felt guilty encroaching on such happiness, but she had no other recourse. She had no intention of crying, but upon seeing Lorna holding her beautiful baby, her eyes welled up with tears that then rolled down her cheeks. She placed the ring and the Bible in Lorna's hands with the request that Jeral receive them if she did not make it out of the surgery alive. The symbols of love and commitment felt like cement in Lorna's hands. She inhaled, exhaled, and nodded her head in affirmation.

Lorna did not realize the extent of Lurline's troubles. She looked at the Bible and ring in her hands and in that moment realized how much she had come to appreciate her newfound friendship. Lurline had one more request for Lorna, which was to read her favorite scripture, Psalm 35. As the anesthesia traveled through Lurline's body, Lorna's words misted through the air. A few filtered through Lurline's consciousness: "Plead my cause, Oh Lord…"

It was Wednesday, April 15th — two days after Lorna had given birth to her little girl — when life was once again celebrated. Two lives reigned: the life of the woman who thought she was going to die in order for her son to live and a male infant who weighed thirteen pounds. He was the talk of the ward; never in the history of the hospital had there been a baby of such great weight. Sewn up with stitches, aching from her surgery, and unable to sit up or move about freely, Lurline rested beside her new friend Lorna. Lurline had such a traumatic delivery that she needed time to heal. My mother, Lorna, rocked, cuddled, and sang to both babies — me, Kadine, and my childhood playmate, my teenage lover, and now husband of ten years — Ontonio. Together we entered the world, and together we explored the mysteries of life beyond picturesque Jamaica.

Chapter Two

I AM LISTENING

*"Their stories; they run through my
thoughts like blood through my veins."*

My parents were great storytellers. They were maybe descendants of the Griots in West Africa who gathered community afore fire, chronicled the village's history, and narrated in detail the challenges and triumphs of their ancestral life cycles. The Griots told stories with passion, exaggeration, and intonation — the rise and fall of voices accompanied by the crackling of fire. It would be these stories, laden with resilience and lightened with humor, that would sustain, light the candle of hope, and keep them humming through the myriad faces of enslavement. Like the fire near their feet, stories kept their souls somewhat warm. This type of storytelling was passed on to my parents, who added their own flair. They each had different ways of delivering their tales in an effort to sear meaning into the psyche of listeners.

My mother's lineage must have been from a tribe whose philosophy one-upped the adage, It takes a village to raise a child, and instead declared, It takes an excruciatingly lengthy story to raise a child well. Like her Sunday morning prayers that stretched on for a solid twenty-one minutes, her stories have always been wordy. After blazing a maze of thought trails and marking each one generously with pauses and verbal pegs for vital points, she would eventually revisit each point, connect the trails, and mastermind a cohesive story — usually a life lesson being her intent.

One of my favorite stories was from my mother's childhood; it spoke of the connection she had with her siblings and how there are consequences to all of our actions. My mother was from a family of fifteen mouths and prone to sharing spaces too small and never enough food to rid her of hunger. To ensure their famishing would be less, she and her brother Lee hatched a plan. It was less suspicious if a girl stayed in the kitchen, and so my mother watched as the salted water simmered at first and then came to a rapid boil. It was the dumplings, the neatly rounded dough that floated atop the bubbling water, that my mother waited for.

When the dumplings floated atop, a sure sign

they were cooked, she whistled a broken tune and Lee appeared with an old Milo can in his hand. Using the lid as a ladle, Lee would scoop two dumplings from the pot. To avoid detection, the siblings would frolic. They kept the steam-infused can from burning either of them by quickly tossing the can to and fro as in a game of catch. They had escaped many times before. Once they reached a clearing beneath the shelter of banana trees, they would sit and share the dumplings equally. They chewed the hot dumplings with half-opened mouths to release some of the steam. Once, Lee tossed the Milo can beyond range, and my mother overreached to catch it. A rusted barb wire caught the flesh of my mother's leg and tore at her skin, ripping it open like an old rag. She wears a scar, a reminder that our actions will always catch up to us.

To me, my mother served as an honorary professor of Never Forgetting Where She Planted Her Pegs. Her memories, a well-worn labyrinth of stories, trailed inward to tales narrated by her parents and the members of her community. She was certainly not immune to the call of dramatics.

Channeling the late Jamaican folklorist Louise Bennett, my mother orated folktales impressed upon her in primary school. Swaying her body to music heard in distant memory, she dressed each word in the rhythmics of her mother tongue: "John Kunno sey him pray fi life, caus fedda will come one day." When the stories belonged to her, the brown of her skin softened and her eyes brightened. As for the words that left her mouth, they journeyed through the canal of our ears, leading us like warm hands into the settings of her life as a child. On my birthday she would meander from teaching lessons, and tell me a well-anticipated age-appropriate — usually perverse — joke.

My twenty-first birthday joke was the best one yet. It had all the fixings of humanity's struggle with desire, monogamy, and sexuality. It was a joke about my father, who as a young man had a knack for sowing his wild oats in "fields" that weren't his own. Often, these "fields" were supposed to be tended by old men, but they had grown weary, leaving their "fields" to be consumed by weeds. Dehydrated and unkempt, it would take a young man — my father — to water and plow such "fields" in secret.

My father was more of a comedian. I truly believe his lineage took the old adage Work hard, then play harder to the next level. Daddy grew up during the Rum Bar Era, a time in which men — and a very few women — gathered at a one-room bar. They listened to the melodies of seventies reggae, drank rum, and shared risque stories. My father's stories were not fit for children; they often caused great conflict in my mother's response. She was, after all, a mother driven to guard our minds, and a woman drawn to the captivating voice of a true storyteller. She would reprimand him while blushing beneath the brown of her skin.

My father's stories derived from his experiences as a young man finding his way in the world at the impressionable age of twelve. His stories were often unclothed.

Complex. Real and raw. My mother would sometimes wink, nudging him to put skirts on his jokes. One truism of our time declares that the greatest comedians — the givers of laughter as medicine — are in fact the ones who carry the deepest pain. I truly believe it was so for my father. Instead of being fed milk as a child, my father told us stories about being fed salted pot water and finding raw potatoes to eat. He left home at the age of twelve because of his father's abuse. According to my father, his mother took the blows of her husband's fist during the day and retreated into his affectionate arms at night.

When my father left home, he did so with a grumbling belly and the clothes on his back. He learned the trade of carpentry from his uncle Busta, "ah likkle dis and ah likkle dat" from men at the bar, and lovemaking from older women. He would be the first to tell you that people are as kind as they are shitty and that all his dearly beloved friends were indeed assholes. He made a song out of the latter and sang it like an anthem when he mounted the eighteen gray steps up to the second floor of our home in Newark, New Jersey. He jangled the bundle of keys he carried as a makeshift instrument. He was a dancing man; sometimes it was his gyrating that added an extra oomph to his stories.

As though I were standing now amidst the crowd gathered in our backyard for a party my father is hosting, I can feel the energy of the people — some whispering in ears, some telling tall tales while sipping on rum punch, and a few holding the necks of Heineken bottles between their fingers. My father stands and the voices hush; a dented circle forms around him. He winks at me and my siblings and begins to tell a story: The Case of Nafty. Nafty, my father begins, was a real fool.

Nafty, my father weaves on, had migrated from Jamaica to the United States in later years as a middle-aged man. He was illiterate, but that didn't stop him from getting a license and driving the roads of Irvington, New Jersey, with the confidence only a Jamaican can muster. He was pulled over by police one too many times, and was caught red-handed holding a spliff as if all was right with his actions. The cops arrived at the car window and were overwhelmed with the scent of ganja. When Nafty received a subpoena, he invited his friends to court. He wore a light blue three-piece suit and a pair of dark blue shoes with tassels. When the bailiff asked him to put his right hand on the Bible and swear to tell the truth and nothing but the truth, Nafty placed his left hand on the Bible, then his right. He continued this for a while until he started twisting his legs to match his hands — a mash-up of salsa and ska ensuing. The people in the courtroom laughed uncontrollably to the point where they could hardly discern the judge's unsteady bang of the gavel. A few chuckles escaped from the judge, who was also being distracted by this grown man who dared to disrupt his courtroom by dancing the Macarena.

My father has captivated his audience. The dented circle of onlookers is enraptured by my father's boisterous voice and the character of Nafty. Everyone laughs. Some slap their knees and the shoulders of their neighbors, others tilt their heads back to hold joy-tears from their eyes. My father waits for the perfect pause, then he continues: "The poor bastard didn't know his left hand from his right." The backyard swells again with merriment. My father's intentions were clear: keep the vibes alive, the cheeks high, the teeth showing, and the belly balled up in stitches. He accomplished this each time he had an audience.

My parents were great storytellers, each of them passing on to me the legacy of heeding the lessons but never forgetting to pause and laugh. I have heard their stories; they run through my thoughts like blood through my veins. As I grow older I realize how much their stories — and they themselves — have shaped me into the woman I am. My style is definitely a mash-up of my mother and my father. From my mother, I have taken the art of placing interjections and nuances into my own story-telling. I tell the tales told to my mother by her mother, the ones I now narrate to my children. Like my father, I learned early about the frailties and complexities of humanity. He was the man who taught me we are all dual citizens residing in one body. I have stored my father's stories on the shelf of my heart. I am waiting for each of my children's birthdays, when I will take a story from the shelf and tell an age-appropriate and most likely perverse joke as my mother did for me and my siblings. It will have all the fixings of humanity's struggle with desire, monogamy, and sexuality. It's a joke, I now know, not just about my father, but the caprices of human nature.

Chapter Three

SEEKING TO FIND

"My parents' connection was the pull of youthful need and the mystery of desire."

I was the only baby in Mass Farkie's one-room rum bar, perched like a bird atop my father's shoulders. My bare feet dangled on his youthful chest and my ears were opened to the ramblings of men who had consumed a copious amount of rum. Their feet no longer moved with the rhythmic skank of island men, but instead stuttered beneath them, buckling into a fall. This was how I spent my Saturday afternoons. Come Sunday, I was the cute and chunky little girl dressed in a frock of frills, skin shining from Vaseline, and smelling of baby powder. I sat beside my mother on the pews of Mount Olivet Church, absorbing the hallelujahs and amens of the island's faithful. My first social atmospheres were as diametrical as my parents.

My mother was a religious, Bible-believing, church-going, Holy Ghost-filled woman who ate her share of the Daily Bread from the Holy Book — preferably the King James Version. My father, on the other hand, was worldly, open to life outside the reach of the

Holy rod, and more likely to be filled with liquid spirits than a ghostly kind. My parents' connection was the pull of youthful need and the mystery of desire. The Bible and the bar would continually remain the biggest contention in my parents' relationship. They wed at my grandparents' countryside home in June of 1981 — two months after I was born. According to the church and Jamaican traditions, I was born a bastard child. I felt nothing of the sort.

My mother moved into my father's house in Walderston, an elongated town ruggedly chiseled out of the mountains in Manchester, Jamaica. It was a one-road-in-and-out kind of town. Drivers beeped their horns rounding corners, swiftly dodging potholes and gullies, and pulling over just in the nick of time to let others pass. The road was bordered by slates of white limestone on either side where houses, invisible to untrained eyes, were tucked into its crevices. Others, like our tiny cerulean house stilted on steel poles and encased in floral cinder blocks, were hanging off the precipice of the mountain. My early childhood home was my father's first canvas. He envisioned, then created a work of art that was envied by our neighbors. He built everything for the house, including an inside bathtub and face basin made of block, cement, and steel. The familial joke remains that my father would have made a couch out of concrete if he had remained on the island.

It was like him to do things differently. He took the path less traveled by becoming a farmworker, traveling and working for six months off the island. His contracts took him to either upstate New York, where he picked apples, or to the snake-infested fields of Florida, where he chopped sugar canes and picked oranges. After his contract ended he returned home to my mother. My father's family was baffled that he chose my mother, whose skin was dusted with cocoa, to be his life partner. They could not see through his eyes how her skin was reminiscent of a moonlit walk, her laughter medicine for his abused heart, and her curves a stimulant for dormant desires.

On his visits home, my father would take me to

the rum bar. While it was an uncommon place for a child, no one dared tell my father so. The fabric of his personality was woven with alternating threads of charm and temper. He was as endearing as he was erratic. The people at the bar had come to respect my father over the years. They admired the tenacity of a young man who envisioned and constructed his home.

He was also a hard worker. With each trip from the States, he added some steel here, a cement block there, and eventually a house was built. It may have helped that he would "buy out the bar," offering each man a choice spirit. On each return, he also brought with him foreign rituals of raising beer bottles and shot glasses in the air and meeting in the middle, offering up a silly toast: "If this drink was a bird, we would call it Swallow." The cold of the Red Stripe ran like a gushing river down their throats; the burst of heat from a shot of rum warmed them. The spirits turned their minds into a melting morass of emotions. Truths laced delicately between lies slurred off tongues. When they became intoxicated, they were free to tell their tales. I became drunk from their stories. It was probably from the drunkards who spilled the deepest, darkest details of their lives that I have come to know our human stories are intricately woven: bestial yet beautiful. After the night of drinking, he carried me home to my mother. I slept in the sweet ignorance of childhood, and woke for church on Sunday morning.

There is a particular image of my childhood im-printed across my mind. I am five years old. The heat of the day has penetrated the red floor beneath me, and I am unbothered, sitting between my mother's thighs, safe, and happy. My mother is grooming me: raking her fingers through the strands of my hair and rubbing castor oil on my scalp. I have been meticulously washed and moistur-ized with Vaseline. The whiff of powder is all over me and I can sense the ruffled panties on my backside under my frilly dress. It's Sunday, the day I attend church with my mother. As we walk down the hill, neighborhood women and children, dressed in Sunday's best, join us. Women are adorned in well-pressed dresses, and wide-brimmed hats with mesh cascading over one eye. The women are ready to offer high praises, worship, and welcome the raining of blessings. Most men stay home to sleep off the night's liquor. The few who attend church are primped in pants with creases as stiff as the persona of righteousness they've tried on but cannot quite fit.

Unlike in the bar, where truth and lies are given voice, congregants hold their words hostage. Instead, they lash their tongues to an unfamiliar language and try to climb to heights of spirituality. Some men and women, caught up in the "spirit," lose control of their bodies and then they flap around on the ground, losing their hats and crushing their clothes. Those who are not in the "spirit" cover them with white sheets to keep the women's under-garments from showing. I watch and listen intently from my place of safety and warmth, wondering why they are fluttering on the floor and to whom they are talking so loudly. The church remains my mother's higher ground, and the bar was my father's place of peace.

Chapter Four

WIDE OPEN-CLOSED

*"The light had not overcome the
darkness where his hand beneath the
table grazed my legs. It was a subtle
graze — one so simple I could have
questioned its actuality. "*

I have a knack for creating and gravitating towards small, enclosed spaces. In these spaces my seating position is back against the wall, face forward, and on alert at all times. But I also yearn for attachment. I adore apothecary pieces of furniture, how compartmentalized they are, yet how fully connected each drawer is to a greater structure. I delight in homes with private, enclosed, or even detached spaces like a garage, guest house, or, as in my own unquenched childhood fantasy, a treehouse high above the ground. I am soothed by the idea of a treehouse... apart from, yet still connected to life below, to a unit, a family, a community.

This is the paradox within me. My desire to be amongst people and indulge in their kinetic energy is strong, while at the same time people scare me. It was the sear of early separation from my mother that gave rise to my paradox. It is sheer grace that does not allow the memory of my grandmother prying my six-year-old body from my mother's arms. She was migrating to the United States, leaving me, my four-year-old sister, and my nine-month-old brother, who was not yet old enough to understand the power of his feet. My father's migration years earlier was softened by my mother's constant presence. But my mother's leaving uprooted me from my primary school, the church at Mount Olivet, and from our home in Walderston. She entrusted our care to our grandparents — Mama and Papa — in the Cumberland District and left to join my father in the pursuit of The American Dream. Four cousins would have the same fate, and they too, with tiny holes in their hearts and the imprints of future struggles with abandonment, joined us when their parents — my maternal aunt and uncle — migrated as well. Mama and Papa's house was already full, but they did not know how to say no to those in search of a home.

In 1988 Gilbert, the ruthless hurricane, devastated the entire island — twisting foundations, scattering board homes beyond their purview, flailing zinc roofs to and fro in the air like drunken birds. My grandparents' home was one of the three that remained. It was a humble home, seven rooms, a long veranda on the front, an outside kitchen off to the side. It had no indoor plumbing. I grew accustomed to filling my bucket with water from the tank in our backyard and towing it to one of the two inside rooms allotted for washing red dirt from my body. When the cock crowed in the mornings, we rubbed the sleep from our eyes and walked through the sounds of crickets and toads to the pit toilet in the middle of the coffee field. We carried newspapers with us, rubbing them back and forth against our palms to soften their effects on our buttocks. When we did not have newspapers, we used the wisdom our grandmother taught us about the herbs and the leaves that would faithfully spring from the earth and be gentle against our flesh. When it was night, we were afforded the luxury of a chimney — a piss pot — that had to be emptied first thing in the morning of its rancid mix of everyone's piss. Our humbleness did not stop my grandparents from welcoming the stream of people who flooded our home during the hurricane.

For several days we all sat in the dark eating tinned foods — cold mackerel, corned beef, and sardines. We ate bread, and we slid our hands through thin slithers of zinc to pick up grapefruits and oranges tossed off the trees by heavy winds. Though we had little drinking water, buckets were placed beneath holes in our roof and water drip-dropped throughout the day, growing louder as sunset darkened our space. We closed our dried lips and weary eyelids. My grandparents' house stood, offering shelter, but it was my grandmother more than my grandfather who did not know how to say no to those seeking refuge. The hurricane was simply the most recent occasion for her offerings.

There were always offers of mercy and shelter. I have an early memory of going on a day trip to Milk River Bath, a spring in Clarendon. We arrived early and played all day long with a young girl, about eight years old at the time — not a parent in sight. When we were packing up to leave, she cried and begged my grandmother to take her with us. My grandmother asked the young girl for directions to her house. Uncle Donovan, my grandmother's fourteenth son, drove the rusty pick-up truck, stripped of its original color by the island sun, over a hill, around a corner, and beside a gully. We dodged tree branches and held our bellies when the potholes made us queasy. When we arrived at the tiny one-bedroom shack, the young girl's parents were sitting on a stoop, a haze of smoke clouding their faces, and the smell of marijuana, pungent. The exchange of words is now a distant memory, fading like smoke in the air. However, I do remember a young girl — a stranger — coming home that night to live with us.

My grandparents were naively hospitable. They grew coffee shrubs and fruit trees, fed stray cats and dogs, and housed those who were in need of a home, some of whom hid their predatory behaviors behind smiles. An older cousin, fifteen years my senior, had appeared and remained with us forever, it seemed. His face offered a sense of calm, but his presence churned within me a contorted discomfort. His words were spoken in a hushed tone, almost a whisper, and his eyes were mirthless. His presence raised, for the time, my awareness of something eerie. I was rankled by both his eyes and his lips that curved at the edges like bent truths. In exchange for room and board, he had been given certain tasks: tilling the soil of my grandfather's field during the day, locking the doors, chaining the grills, and lighting the kerosene lamps at night. It was already dark the first night he lit the lamp and placed it on the table. The orange flames with shimmers of blue flickered behind the hourglass shape, bouncing light onto the walls.

The light had not overcome the darkness where his hand beneath the table grazed my leg. It was subtle — a movement so simple I could have questioned its actuality. When I looked, his countenance was an apologetic question mark and his lips parted themselves in a conniving grin. Perplexed, I sat unaware of the danger ahead. If only I had allowed the undercurrent of fear within me to take center stage, the darkness to come might have disappeared in the lamp light. But I answered his gaze with silence — giving him an opening, a cracked window into tormenting me.

He seemed always present. The open fields where I once played fearlessly became a battleground — far too large for my young eyes to scan. The security of yester-year no longer enveloped me. The days of being carefree had been lifted and worry laced its arms around me in its stead, forcing me to play with caution. I did nothing in peace. I polished the red floor, then pushed and pulled the coconut brush across the veranda with the fear of him as a shadow looming over me. He was like an eyelash falling: I never saw or felt him coming. He popped out of places I usually went to play hide-and-seek with my cousins. He lay in wait for me at the little pit toilet in the coffee field — not even shitting deterred him. He sought after me, escalating from the barest of touches to wrestling me to the ground. His attempts became more frequent and he was less selective on his points of attack. His eyes peered strangely out at me, like some uncanny version of adult peek-a-boo.

One late afternoon in the fields, he grabbed my arm. His palm was clammy when it caught my wrist, and forced me to the ground. I could smell his body — a rancid mix of grass, dirt, and sweat. When he tried to pull my dress over my head, I kicked my legs aiming to hurt and sank my teeth into his flesh aiming to draw blood. I ran. I tasted his dirty flesh as my tiny eight-year-old feet trampled the grounds and destroyed the flowers in my path. I found refuge in the woodlands above our house and sat on a patch of red dirt beneath a tree. I was exhausted. I waited for my mind to realize I was free, but it would take years for my spirit and my mind to meet. When my grandmother started talking of my siblings and me reuniting with our parents, I decided to keep my mouth closed and wait to be safe — high above in the treehouse of the United States, and the embrace of my parents' arms.

Chapter Five

SISTERS

"There was indeed much to discuss as each took turns sharing, listening, offering advice or insight to the conundrums that had become their lives."

When my siblings and I arrived in the United States in October 1991, we learned that our mother had two birthdays. We celebrated both — March 27 and March 29. The 29th was the date her parents gave her — the date she acknowledged as an important part of her identity. It was not until she received a pig and her birth certificate as wedding gifts that she learned March 27th was her actual date of birth.

My mother makes light of this mishap because, according to her, her older sister Ezzie, the prayer warrior and family historian, has it worse. Ezzie remains uncertain whether she was born in January or June. It is like my mother to placate her pain with pleasantries. It is her method of coping with the gravity of having to find the sunshine behind the shadows and faith in the foolish. It is a habit she found useful even as a child.

My mother and her family moved to Cumberland on a donkey. Two worn wicker baskets hung on either side of the animal. The basket on the left was stacked with dried grass, covering a hole that cushioned my mother's seven-year-old body. Her brother Lee sat in the other basket and her older siblings played along the path. They took a shortcut through Swamp, a fertile field fit for farming and wild fruit trees bearing rose apples, guavas, and jackfruits. The bustling of wildlife rankled leaves above their heads, and dried sticks scraped legs below. It was in this untamed field that my mother slipped through the hole in the basket, unseen and unheard. She remained there for the hour and a half it took her parents to arrive at their new home and to realize they were missing a child. When they backtracked, they found my mother playing with twigs, her feet awash with red mud, and her mental curtain drawn tight — blocking her view of fear and discomfort.

My mother grew up with thirteen siblings in a three-room house. Her parents shared one room, the girls another, and the boys spilled over into the "living room." In each room, they stuffed individual caya bags with dried leaves for beds on concrete. They slept breaths apart. The cement floor had been turned red with a coat of red oak wax and shined with coconut brushes much like the ones used to clean the veranda floor.

The veranda was covered but not enclosed and its view was an expanse of vegetation. It was there that my mother's sister — a little girl too beautiful to have lived, so the story goes — was buried in a beer box.

My mother's parents obeyed the order of day and night. My grandfather, a dark-skinned man with gentle sapphire eyes, was a man of time. He rose before the cock crowed and could have been the rooster's alarm. He was a man of order. He dressed in a freshly pressed pair of green khaki pants with the crease down the middle that my grandmother ironed the night before. He tucked his shirt in the waist of his pants and belted himself as if due in town instead of heading to his farm to tend yams and potatoes. His black water boots stretched to his knees, shielding his pants legs from early morning dew and the jook of mackas. He tended the land before the high sun and tracked home through the mud to eat whatever my grandmother had prepared for lunch. She would have been home tending to their house, nursing a new baby, and fearing the possibility that she was once again with child. When the sun closed its eyes on their Jamaican countryside abode, they'd retreat behind the walls that kept their secrets of the night.

My grandparents adhered to gender roles as much as they did to the natural rhythm of day and night. My grandfather planted and harvested and my grandmother went to market. On Thursday mornings she, along with other women, crammed into a rickshaw bus. Their harvest of yams and bananas bursting the seams of crocus bags had been tied to the top of the bus, tilting it. After a three-and-a-half-hour ride dodging potholes and missing gullies, they arrived at Carnation Market in Kingston. Once there, the women built their stalls, hung tarps to block the sun, and hollered out what they'd brought with them, hoping to sell all their produce by Saturday night. For the two nights they were there, my grandmother made a cot with banana trash and placed a basket as her pillow.

It was on one of these trips that my grandmother met a woman who frequented her stall. My grandmother was rich in faith and fertility. She was pregnant with my mother — the ninth of her thirteen children. Her friend was barren after making the mistake of washing her belly of a child. They became great friends.

I would like to think it was my grandmother's faith that nudged her to give my mother, who was seven years old, to her barren friend. I still wonder about that decision-making process. Was the question asked? Who dared to breathe life into those words? Did my grandmother blindfold herself, spin around, and point? Did she toss names into a hat and pick at random? Or maybe, just maybe, she pinned my mother's name to the ass of a donkey. Did her friend have a specific child in mind? Was it her request to have a girl versus a boy? Had my mother gone in fear with the stranger? Did my mother's tiny

heart beat at a fast pace beneath her thin clothing of skin?
Memory fails my mother.

She would have remained in the woman's care
except for the actions of one perverted guest. He used
my mother's body as means for his self-seeking satis-
faction. My mother returned home at the age of twelve
— cautious and suspicious. She was determined to find
an escape from the low-grade expectations of women on
the island: housewifery, sex slaves to their husbands, and
breeding — popping out children one year after the other.

My mother did find a way out, and it brought her
to the United States. Years later when we reunited with
her, she gave us her best: her smile birthed from laughter, her voice croaking, waking us in song, and her stories
that went on and on forever. She groomed us on Saturday mornings on the living room floor during the cold
months and in the backyard when spring brought back
the birds and flowers.

My mother is short and stunning, with a small face and a small nose. Her smile is wide and deep, exposing clean white teeth untouched by coffee and red wine. She does not wear pants. All her skirts and dresses are pinched at the waistline, accentuating her breasts, standing as though she had never breastfed a child, much less three. The pinching honors the sway of her hips and the curve of her buttocks, her hemline reaching down to caress her ankles. Growing up, she stayed clear of profanities and remained intact in the face of all that seemed to be falling apart around her: the unfaithfulness of her husband, the mothering of emotionally hormonal children, and the need to assist a few of her siblings.

Her lightest of days came when her three sisters visited from New York. They had all lived with her in New Jersey at one point before becoming enamored by the dazzling lights of the city across the bridge. They took the trips often, leaving the dirty but beloved streets of the Bronx behind. They paid the four-dollar toll to cross the George Washington Bridge, drove down the Parkway and arrived at our home on Aldine Street. The four of them, each in a complex relationship, sat together around our oval table. Laughter spilled out from them. Then hushed conversations moved them to the couch. Like quadruplets in a bassinet they would make their way to the comfort of my mother's queen-size bed — a gift my father had purchased in one of the glory months of his home improvement business.

I remember the day we went to the furniture store. My father was beaming, excited that, finally, he could purchase a new bed for his wife — not a hand-me-down from a thrift store. I remember my mother's eyes scanning the massive warehouse with furniture on display, ultimately landing on the one she wanted and giving my father the look he understood without words. He told the salesperson he wanted it all — the bed, the nightstands, the chest of drawers, the armoire, the lamps, and even the plants that were used to stage the set. While we waited for furniture to be delivered, my father installed a soft white carpet and hung sheer white curtains that let in the breeze and the sunlight. My mother's room was her own Shangri-La.

When the sisters migrated from the table to my mother's bed, they took turns sharing, listening, and offering advice for the conundrums that had become their lives. It was a far cry from the fantasies that had twirled in their heads about the great American Dream. However, there was a sense of gratitude from knowing how far they had traveled — not just in distance, but in quality from the destitutions of a third-world country.

The sisters understood how far they had come but fear did not evade them. They had heard the horror stories of deportation and exploitation of the undocumented. They were unlicensed, driving afraid, quivering with fear and collapsing into relief at the passing of a police vehicle. To live, they wiped sloppy noses and old white asses, cleaned floors and toilets, loaned and borrowed names as easily as they did money. As time went on, they celebrated each letter from Homeland Security, each green card in the mail, each passport, and every other milestone that made them feel free in America. They had done it all together, learning to be vulnerable and letting each other in.

Chapter Six

FALLING

*"Fear squatted heavily on our chests,
forcing tears onto our cheeks and
silently down our faces onto our hands
clutched below."*

Guilt, like its companion, fear, can be a strong tox-icant that sinks into our thoughts and dreams. I have had — without fail — three recurring dreams. In one I am no longer the Jamaican who is gawked at for not knowing how to swim. Instead, my non-aquatic body is the ocean. I am the tempestuous wave and I am the gentle water cleansing sand from bare feet. In another dream, I am above in the heavens resting on air, floating like clouds and creatures of flight. My eyes are feasting on green pas-tures, silver water, and mountains dressed in white. I fly over all of them, free and light. I go with ease into these worlds: into the ocean and up in the skies. These dreams speak of the dichotomy in my reality.

The third dream is the uprooting of all I know. This dream has me neither flying nor swimming; I am be-tween ocean and sky. I am here on earth, and it is a dream I dread. I had a relative whose hands — when he hugged me — would slip to the slight indent of my back, right at the mount of my ass. He was a sneaky bastard because it would be right when his wife turned her back. He was the creepy constant of my reality, just like my third dream is a creepy constant in my subconscious.

The dream begins with a slight opening of my lips, gently pulling my cheeks up towards my eyes, revealing my teeth. I stand in this moment the epitome of beauty, a group of onlookers pleased by the sight of me. I can feel them, but my eyes cannot see the faces they wear. It is then that one of my molars is uprooted and shatters, each particle agitating — with the slightest touch — the teeth that remain. All my teeth uproot and burst into tiny pieces, causing an avalanche in my mouth. In my dream, my lips perform their own desperate act of preservation, pressing tightly together to seal my mouth. My lips fail, and just before the bedrock of teeth and streams of blood spill out, I awake in terror, afraid and trembling. I glide my tongue across my gums, desperate to find my teeth intact. I am shaken and my insides become a mess of molten fear.

It is alarming how a dream can feel so real and invasive. This third dream made me feel anxious, desperate, and powerless. The dream was a small window into my reality. It had been one of my best-kept secrets. It was not one I shared freely because of my upbringing with superstitious Jamaicans. They claimed such a dream could only mean disgrace and utter embarrassment to those who had the misfortune of being related to me. My teeth had always afforded me a brilliant smile. Hidden beneath it was the paradox of a happy but fearful child. I was afraid of being rejected, left behind...again.

After five years with our maternal grandparents, we were smuggled into a new country in the cold of winter. The warmth of our parents' arms was a joyous and jarring experience. My emotions ran from hot to cold as I lingered in the middle ground of expectancy and uncertainty. For the years we were apart, we had become distinctive entities: the two of them and the three of us — my sister, my brother, and me. We became a family of five, each person an unexplored world of wounds and wonder.

Our parents put their present selves upon a shelf and shared stories of a time past. They told us of the early years when they planned their lives with the air only youth can embrace. It was decided my mother would tend the house and children while my father axed himself in two. Half the year he was a farmworker and bachelor in the United States, unencumbered by wife and children. The other half he lived in Jamaica, a married man.

His comings and goings affected us all. Though I did not understand at the young age of three, I could sense his departures — maybe because in my memory his leavings were foretold with a slight undertone of sadness encased in music. I remember clearly our little blue house being consumed with the pining of Percy Sledge, crying his soul out about "When a Man Loves a Woman," and the late reggae artist John Holt intoning an invitation to "Lay Your Head on My Pillow." I suppose, in retrospect, my parents were both laying their heads on a pillow, trying to fuel each other's eroticism for the bitter, lonely months ahead when my father would fly off to America.

My father's eyes were newly opened to the pipe dreams farmworkers were sold — inhumanity adorned as opportunity. Shy of squeezing their muscles like shoppers squeeze melons to assess acceptability, American companies picked Jamaican men based on physical fitness. My father told stories about fit men who received on-the-job injuries. A worker not properly trained to use a large tractor ran over another worker. The driver heard the worker's cry. He tried to back up but instead drove the tractor over him again. The man's legs and ribs were broken. He received minimal care from the company's doctor, then was flown home with minimal compensation, and given a false promise of being re-signed. My father realized Jamaican men were disposable.

After several years of working and seeing the disrespect bosses had for the work he and others did, my father planned his escape. He would "run off," risking imprisonment and deportation. My father lived as an illegal immigrant for about three years, until he was granted amnesty under the Immigration Reform and Control Act of

1986. My father had the freedom to roam, and roam he did, even after my mother arrived in New Jersey the first day of 1987.

My parents' marriage was turbulent, adorable, and real. I have vivid memories of my parents greeting each other. I can hear my father whistling his way up the eighteen steps to our home on the second floor. My mother sashays her way over to the door to greet him. They are both standing beneath an exposed light bulb turned on and off by a long dangling string. He's bending his knees and long torso to meet my mother's smiling face, reaching his hands around her thighs, and pulling her up so his strong arms become a chair for her derriere. Her feet are suspended just beneath my father's knees. Their faces meet and as they come eye to eye, their lips half open — as though rehearsed — invite the other in for a taste. I surmise my father would whisper something decadent in my mother's ear because she would fold her face into his neck and shake with laughter. My father was an enigma for my mother; he was the source of her ease and cause of her burden.

With the exception of their common stance on education, my parents had varying ideologies, especially about our family life. While my mother worked under the table as a nanny during the day, she was normally home by six o'clock. My father, on the other hand, had plans to be elsewhere. He would grace us with his presence for dinner. However, immediately following he would leave for his reign as vibes man at the pool hall and return only after we had gone to bed — sometime late in the early morning hours. It was not the jingling of his keys that would summon us to his arrival. Instead, it was my mother's muffled litany of irritation and my father's soothing answers. My mother would laugh under his whispers and he would win her over and over again.

Underneath my mother's calm exterior, there was unexpressed contention that turned into dizzy spells and fainting. She grew physically ill. The first few times my mother fainted, I called an ambulance, but its arrival proved unnecessary. Minutes before its flashing lights and sirens turned the corner onto Aldine Street, my mother regained consciousness. She clasped the task she had left hanging in midair and continued as if nothing had happened. After a while, we created protocols for such instances: I held her head on my lap and fanned her face aggressively while my sister or brother drenched a rag with cold water and wiped her face. We fanned, wiped, and repeated until she was back with us on our side of the light. The life force was being leached from my mother because of her determination to make my father a homebody. She wanted him to stay home, engage us in conversation, and go to church with us on Sundays. She pursued. He protested. We watched. She snapped.

The conversation began like any ordinary exchange. At its worst, it would have warranted my mother kissing her teeth to dismiss him. However, because my mother had clenched her thoughts and stifled her words for the sake of peace for so long, she was tightly woven and the conversation escalated into an argument in a matter of minutes. Heated words raised the temperature to a point beyond boiling when the booty of victory became the children. My father fumed out the words he would live to regret: "You will get my kids over my dead body!" His words were like a dark smoke that covered her face. When the smoke cleared, my mother had disappeared. The caregiver and nurturer of our household had evaporated into a mist high above, probably shaking her head at her alter ego which had taken her place below. The woman who reappeared wore my mother's face and body, but not her temperament. As though she had signed a deal with the machete god, she gripped the machete in her right hand. She held it, pulled it back to gain momentum, and fueled it forward. It was fortune that shut my eyes from the impact of steel upon beloved flesh, but there was no grace guarding my ears. I heard the CHINK of steel against ceramic. I opened my eyes to my father's face twisted in horror, his wrist dangling, blood pouring and pooling in a crimson puddle on the white tiles. My mother then reclaimed her body and in a voice as delicate as yellow butterflies' wings gave us all directives, my father included.

I was to get a towel to soak up blood. Upon my return, she was holding his injured hand in one of hers, and stretching the other out towards me in silent urgency for the towel. She wrapped his wrist with tenderness, and as though she feared her voice could harm us, she spoke softly: Get your boots, put on your coat, and get in the car. For all the times we had driven together, we all knew our places without query. However, my parents changed seats that night. My father sat awkwardly in the passenger seat, unable to adjust, clutching his injured hand, his knees digging into his chest. My mother, on the other hand, quickly adjusted her new seat to accommodate her short legs. She made a quick left, a sharp right, and another left onto Lyons Avenue.

The mood inside the car resembled the darkness of the night, the only illumination coming from the lights lining the street. I noticed dust dancing lightly under the street lamps, making a polka-dot gleam on the ground wet from the pitter patter of rain. In our car, fear squatted heavily on my chest, forcing tears onto my cheeks, and silently down my face. As we pulled into emergency parking at Beth Israel Hospital, my father's words remained trapped beneath his tongue. My mother became the storyteller. She whispered a tale to the nurses who continually probed about the night's unfolding. Only my mother answered, repeating the same tale at every asking. The truth was not revealed that night.

Like the teeth of my recurring dream, my parents' life together was fractured. We had sat together, alone within ourselves, in the cold emergency room of the hospital. My father bleeding, our family breaking, and all of us falling apart.

Chapter Seven

BIG DADDY

"We learned quickly to quell the questions of his return; he would return only when he grew tired of the night."

There was no time to focus on my parents' marital issues, we were fighting for the restoration of my father's body.

There is a picture of my father standing slightly off-kilter, wearing a fedora hat tipped to the side, a white fishnet vest, and '80s unisex sports shorts. His body is a statue of masculinity — muscles and veins intertwined. For the rare nights he stayed home and prepared for bed, he wore a striped navy and white nightshirt, the words BIG DADDY embroidered on it. As for the other nights, when he left my mother, sister, brother, and me at home and headed out to play cards, dominoes, and pool at the bar, he dressed seamlessly. To avoid his own unease with answering pesky questions about his evening whereabouts, he narrated his plans by laying his clothes out on his bed. A pressed suit still covered in clear plastic revealed a caped wire hanger holding his shirt and a strut holding his pants. Atop he would add a bolo to match and a gentleman's shoes of linen or leather set on the carpet beneath. It was his philosophy that jeans and anything besides linen or leather shoes were for pussies. When he was all dressed, his suit sat on him as trenchantly as his weekly haircut — its edges acute as his wit. We learned quickly to quell the questions of his return; he would return only when he grew tired of the night.

My father had ignored the internal warnings of his diseased body, and the illness was finally revealing itself externally. His body was losing its tall, lean, and muscular stature. His feet had ballooned in size, appearing as though, with the prick of a pin, water would come rushing from them. His belly grew, mimicking the early bulge of a woman in her second trimester, or of a snake that had just swallowed a large egg. The whites of his eyes had taken on a dirty red and yellow hue, as though they were both jaundiced and bleeding. I noticed his eyes one evening after he had reversed his white van. I was closing the gate behind him when our eyes met. It was akin to wading through murky waters, summoning within me a sense of panic — a sudden trembling in my feet that could only be felt, not seen. We both paused, befuddled affections lying dormant beneath our roles as parent and child. He paused the painful pause of a parent wondering where time had gone; and in that moment I recognized that my father was dying.

It reminded me of a summer when he was building the three-car garage in the backyard and sneaking cigarette breaks. Though we knew he smoked, he had never wanted us to see him doing so and had actually warned us against picking up habits we would struggle to put down. My siblings and I had planned to catch him in the act. We watched and waited. Just as he lit the Marlboro, we pushed our heads through our second-floor bedroom window overlooking the backyard. As swiftly as he could, he pulled the lit cigarette behind his back and we were in a head-to-head battle. We tried to engage him in conversation, and he tried to make us retreat inside by reminding us of a chore undone. We prevailed. The cigarette fumed in space behind him, creating a burning trail. When the flame singed his fingers, he dropped the cigarette, stomped it out, and shook his hand against the unfounded cool of a New Jersey summer. Risible, he looked up at us, and clothed — motherfucker! — in humor. He was sick now, aflame like the cigarette he failed to hide, burning at a speed unseen, slowing into ash.

My mother had known he was sick for several months. She said and did all she could to convince him to see a doctor. She pulled out the sakes cards: for the kids' sake, for my sake, for your sake, and for Jesus Christ's sake. She climbed the stairs from the ground floor of gentle reminders, rode the escalator of threats and bribes, and finally took the elevator to the one persuasion that had worked with him, and us kids, many times before: malice. She withdrew, an art form she had practiced and mastered. When we pissed her off, she held her words captive for days; and a few times she held them in bondage for weeks. My father's stiff-neckedness, however, had her beat. His reluctance was fueled by his personal mistrust of preachers and doctors. In my father's opinion, trying to convince him to see either was dismissed with a rise of his brow. He often declared, "Doctors ask dumb questions, then take your money; preachers are pimps who preach panties off the women of the church."

His feet grew to the ticking of a clock — a size larger each hour. By one o'clock in the afternoon, his feet prevented him from walking long distances or standing for any reasonable amount of time. His leather and linen shoes no longer fit his once-slender feet. My mother bought him a white pair of Dr. Scholl's sneakers, the ones with both laces and Velcro. My father laughed from a clenched heart, obscenities escaping with the heartbeat that came each time he caught his breath. He laughed from sheer panic, not delight. His feet — his means of transportation into forbidden delights — were failing him. No longer could they take him to the places that satisfied his social cravings for cigarettes, drinks, cards, and playing pool. They could no longer stand under the gravity of his heavy, diseased body. Sneakers would be a total contradiction to his style. It was time to see the asshole — the doctor my mother had researched and recommended months earlier.

When my parents returned home that evening, they both coerced a smile to hide the new hollowness growing in the center of their beings. My father was diabetic and had gone untreated for at least two years. There was no time to plan or prepare. The entire family would join in suffering the powdery nonsense that is Equal, the agony of eating cardboard called wheat flour, and the denial of salt, pepper, and spice. Our taste buds rebelled, our throats stood guard against bland assault by the diabetic menu, and we swallowed only by force. My father learned to disconnect himself from the tastelessness of food and laughed instead at our contorted faces. He laughed each time he took his shot of insulin. He made jokes and chortled often, a mind trick maybe for us to forget that he was sick and dying.

From one of his routine doctor's appointments, my father was sent directly to Beth Israel Hospital. He was admitted. Our lives changed again, and we all adjusted. After school, my sister and I would get off the bus and meet my brother and mother at the hospital. I'm still not certain how my mother did it all, but she went to work and then would be at the hospital before we arrived, with dinner in a thermos and juice in any container that had a cover. Together we ate dinner and laughed as my father told jokes about the nurses, the day's unfolding, and about his neighbor with a "stinkin" toe. His exaggerated Jamaican accent made every word funnier. We did our homework while our parents talked in whispers and eye movements. At eight-thirty, when visiting hours were over, we split our family of five — leaving my dad behind, the four of us heading home. Life had grown cold, unnerving, and unfamiliar. The four of us fit tightly on my parents' bed, lingering between two worlds, unsure of either.

On one of our later visits, my father seemed weaker than usual, almost as if he was fighting sedation. It was then we learned he had cirrhosis of the liver from one too many Heinekens and shots of Jamaican rum chased with hot sauce. He would need a liver transplant to survive. His health was declining, but the doctors sold us their hope. We rode the waves of hope, relieved when we learned he was scheduled for surgery the following morning. The plan was clear: Daddy would have the surgery in April and attend my high school graduation in June.

It was around one a.m. when the home phone rang, breaking the silence of the night and waking us from sleep. The nurse told my mother to come. We went mute as we gathered in the dark, clothed ourselves in light jackets, and hope. My mother drove silently to the hospital and we walked through the hallway in an eerie trance-like state. We were directed away from the room we had come to know, down a much longer hallway with brighter lights, colder walls, and glossy gray floors. We approached the nurses' station, where a group of them were clustered like grapes, showing all signs of being alive: movement, laughter, and chatter. One of the nurses recognized us and nonverbally sounded the alarm. Some invisible vacuum cleaner above the nurses' heads evaporated their vibrancy. The room hushed, making their secret warning — the family is here — overwhelmingly loud, almost as if it was shouted from a bullhorn.

They all swallowed their smiles, and a somber wand waved over their faces, one right after the other. It was surreal how fast essence changed, how quickly they adjusted to serving us. Truly, nurses are superior beings. They escorted us to a small waiting room. When the doctor arrived a few minutes later, he took a seat before my mother and lowered his head to the ground as though what he had to say was written on the floor. It took him hours, it seemed, to pull his head away from his left shoulder and gently align it at center, finally giving him a posture of which his mother would be proud. He breathed heavily, opened his mouth, and the words, "we're sorry" dripped out in slow-motion. This makes me now think about my love-hate relationship with a few words in the English language. Sorry is one of them. Nothing good ever comes before or after "I'm sorry." He continued, "We tried our best, but we were unable to resuscitate him."

It's strange. We know the truths common to all: we're born to live, we live a while, then we die. But death seems to surprise us. Bad news and death never have good timing. The doctor's words attacked my mother first, slapped my sister and me a few seconds later. My brother, who was twelve at the time, had not understood what was being said. My mother recognized his unknowing face and gently — as though not to crack the floor — walked over to him. Her words trailed off in a whisper, but with the force of a mule, kicked my brother in the back. He fell face forward onto the glossy gray floor. Big Daddy was gone.

Chapter Eight

THE RASTAMAN

"His voice rose and mine vanished."

The reality of our family of five was buried with my father's forty-four-year-old body. While he rested, my mother, sister, brother, and I were left in an upheaval, unable to grasp the magnitude of our loss. We existed only as empty shells, recognizable from skin on the outside but cored on the inside. My sister placed a shield of survivor over her quaking heart, and it would be years before she removed it. My brother balled his anger into a fist and shattered a glass door at school one day. The glass sliced his flesh, split his artery, and created a seven-inch scar. After several months of physical therapy, when his cast was removed, he found peace by drawing for hours while sitting on our living room floor. My mother wore red unmentionables to ward off further sexual advances from my dead father. She found clarity in walking for miles, oftentimes getting lost, and calling home for me to pick her up. The streets of Newark untwined before me, and I would find her, sweating and slightly renewed. I, on the other hand, meandered through the fog of grief and marijuana. After three-and-half years of dating and breaking it off with the American, I fell googly-eyed over the Bahamian.

Shortly after, I met my father's doppelgänger: the Rasta-man.

At the first sight of the Rastaman, my heart moved from the left of my chest and squeezed itself into the right. It did not belong there and would not survive. I took shallow breaths for the two years we dated, created a life, and then a home together. We had not dated long before I was pregnant. I told him the news in the tiny bathroom of my mother's house. He lifted me into his arms, careful not to swing my legs into the sink, the tub, or the toilet. He asked to be with me when I told my mother I was pregnant, but I declined. It would be difficult for me to shatter my mother before someone she barely knew; a man who was yet to reveal himself to me.

I moved out of my mother's house and into a studio apartment the Rastaman found for us. Our apartment was small — the kitchen, living room, and bedroom melted into one. The expanse of a wall-to-wall window harnessed the light, enlarging the feel of our space. We hung black sheer curtains to offer us privacy and to let in glimmers of light that tangoed on the black-stained hardwood floor. Our furniture was minimal: a bed placed by the window, a chest of drawers in front of the bed, a loveseat with a Bob Marley poster hung overhead, a clear coffee table in the center, and on the opposite side of the room, a television was anchored to the wall. The red, yellow, and green Rastafarian flag claimed the spot made empty by the migration of my heart.

The Rastaman was a man of habits and had not once called me by my birth name. Instead, I answered to his interchangeable monikers, Empress or Princess, which I found endearing and intoxicating. I slid into his Rastafarian lifestyle without thought, losing myself like an old snakeskin. I listened to his choice of music — Sizzla, Pressure, and Anthony B. I ate vegetarian foods that he prepared with a passion. The kitchen was a place of ecstasy for him. He tied a white bandanna around his head, Sensei style. He soaked soya chunks, sharpened his knife, julienned carrots and cabbage in one swift move. Water bubbled in one pot, oil sizzled in another; he sprinkled salt, spices, and herbs without measurement. Our apartment was a foodie's paradise. As though he was being rocked with music, he swayed when he tasted the union of vegetables, ground foods, and perfectly crisp sweet plantains. He made Peanut Punch on Saturday mornings — blending unsalted peanuts, oats, cinnamon, vanilla, nutmeg, and Guinness. Sundays he rested and I grew homesick.

It took months before the emotions and cravings of pregnancy created new yearnings within me and reminded me of myself. He condemned the eating of meat. I craved Italian subs and fried chicken. When I was six months pregnant, I ate foods of my likings in secret. I buried the wrappers from the subs in the bottom of the garbage and drove forty-five minutes to the mall to secretly get my chicken fix. I missed my family, especially around Christmas. I missed our traditions — the scent of pine trees, morning worship, the gift exchange, breakfast that flowed into lunch, even our family bicker that would end in laughter. I missed playing games: Monopoly if my sister pleaded long enough, Scrabble if my pleading won, and Jamaican Ludi when my brother won his choice.

The Rastaman did not play games, but like my father, he told stories of his youthful days in Portmore, Jamaica. I grew intrigued by his boyhood on the darker, more dangerous side of the island. He spoke of how he walked the lines of rude boy and Rastafarianism. He rolled out stories of his present life as a cook — the heat in the kitchen, and the funny Americans — all while he rolled and licked the ends of his spliff. He smoked it two times per day. The first would be in the early morning, just after he peeled an orange and placed it on my nightstand. He chanted a psalm from his little blue Bible, beat his congo drum, and raised his spliff to his lips. When the day was done he changed from his white cook's coat into more comfortable clothing — a faded Bob Marley t-shirt and a loose pant cut above his ankles. When he sat on the couch beside our bed, he lifted his locks into a loose bun, revealing his facial features: a charming smile that raised his cheeks and illuminated the brown and crimson freckles on his boyish face. The reddish beard shaping his face resembled that of a young lion. His habits were deeply embedded in his character, and the Rastaman had smoked himself into a split personality. He would raise an unusually large spliff to his lips, close his eyes, and inhale the person I had come to fancy: a calm, funny, gentle soul who sang while he cooked and whose food danced on my palate. Then he exhaled a stranger: a loud and paranoid critic whose voice penetrated the walls of our small studio apartment. My shamefulness grew like my pregnant belly. In the mornings, neighbors with questioning eyes searched my face, my arms, and legs for bruises and scars. I had none on my flesh; they were deeper than any physical markings, and one of them led to our undoing.

A college friend had a baby three months before me, and on one of my visits, she offered me a bag of newborn clothing and a half bag of newborn Swaddlers diapers. I was thrilled to go home and scavenge through the bag of treasures with the Rastaman. However, at the mere mention of the bag, he lashed a stare of disgust across the room. He was angry that I took the clothing, and he was supremely pissed off that I had taken an already open bag of diapers. He was offended that someone would think he could not afford new ones for his own child. I tried explaining that young mothers in America share these items without care because babies grow so quickly. I also tried explaining that she was not pitying us, but his ears were already barricaded with fury. His voice rose and mine vanished. It was almost as if I was in one of those dreams where the words floated in my head, traveled as far as my tongue, but my lips were glued shut.

As though he wanted to wake me from my ignorance, he inhaled and exhaled the words that would send the final blade through me: "Princess," he said, "you are worthless for taking someone's old clothes." I gasped loudly, mourning us. For a quick moment, I was transported into our future and saw his words take on life. Our daughter was five years old in my vision. I could clearly see the impact of his verbal mishandling — my head hanging low, barely looking up, and my daughter's eyes steadfast on me drinking in the poison. The sharpness of his words reached into my heart where the Rastafarian flag had been planted. With one swift pull, I yanked it out.

I knew then our relationship was failing, but it was confirmed a few weeks later after I gave birth to our baby girl. The hospital room was peaceful, dimly lit from the light beaming through the crack under the door. I was waiting for the Rastaman when the nurse brought my baby in for a feeding. She asked my name, checked the name tag on my daughter's leg to make sure the Asian-looking baby belonged to the brown likes of me. I was finally holding my baby in my arms. It was a painful and holy moment when I held her to my engorged breast. The serenity of her feeding was broken by a clear Voice proclaiming: You are going to be alone for a while, but you're going to be okay.

I returned to our apartment two days later, attempting to ignore the shattering of my heart and the words of the Voice. I lay on our bed one night, our daughter in the middle and the Rastaman on the other side — a picture-perfect family. While they slept soundly, I lay wide awake, my head on a pillow of thorns, my back pressing into a mattress of sinking sand, and my nose sticking out as I gasped for air. As though my thoughts were muffled underwater, I got out of bed to think more clearly. Standing upright calmed me to some degree. As scared as I was, the Voice was a source of empowerment. I cried while I packed our bags and cleaned the apartment at three o'clock a.m.

When the Rastaman woke that morning, he greeted me as though the night had not happened. He placed the peeled orange on my nightstand and I told him I was moving out. He laughed and I packed the car. I watched him through the rearview mirror: standing with his arms crossed, his face an open mouth filled with questions I could not hear. The one-way street led me to a stop sign. I made a right, then a left, and two more rights to arrive at the doorstep of my mother's fears: Single. Black. Mother. The Voice had to be right.

Chapter Nine

SACRED SPACE

"Gray waves were swooping over the blue of day joining feathered strokes of orange and silver slashing softly across the sky."

The year before, when I told my mother I was pregnant, I was twenty-two years old and a year shy of completing undergrad. I sat on the carpet next to my mother's bed, terrified of being rejected. Her disappointment was tangible — fear was at the forefront. The weight of the news dragged her chin to her breast. She vacuum sealed herself into a rigid posture: she straightened her back, sealed her lips, and tried with all her strength to keep the tears from falling. My pregnancy shattered the hopes my mother had for my life. I carried my mother's pain, along with my apprehensions, to an encounter with my sister.

My sister and I sat on the edge of the doorway, squished side by side, the tightness of the doorpost holding us in place. Our bond gave me the courage to repeat the words that had just caused our mother such anguish — "I'm pregnant."She leaped to her feet, as though propelled by ten angels and threw her arms of love and acceptance around me. "We're pregnant?" She asked the question in a sing-song voice that filled me with relief. I felt and held the sacredness of the moment.

When our father was still alive, my sister and I sat on the same doorstep one perfect New Jersey spring afternoon. We watched as he held the delicacy of tulip bulbs in his callused hands. He stood on the bit of brown earth between the concrete of our driveway and our neighbors' two-story house. He dug a hole in the earth with his machete, knelt, and planted the bulbs one by one, row by row. The spring day and the earth were medicine. He hummed and smiled to himself. When he caught us looking at him, his eyes warmed and he winked at us. While the garden could only be seen from the neighbors' second-story window and could only be accessed by walking on our driveway, our neighbors had declared it was their land. Tulips — nourishing to the eyes — simply were not allowed. In our absence one day, they uprooted the bulbs from their home in the earth. They tossed the potential of red, pink, and white flowers onto our driveway. The bulbs languished, adrift on an ocean of concrete. My sister and I had watched the earth's transformation: barren, bountiful, and bare again.

My sister and I are eighteen months apart. If combined, we could be the first fully functioning, balanced human being. Separately, we need each other to make sense. I am an emotional dreamer — moving from one state to another, meandering from one experience to the next, gathering data, I suppose, for my life as a writer. She, on the other hand, can be dialed on the same phone number she's had since college. She is pragmatic, career-oriented, and has lived with her sweet family in the same house for the past ten years. She is in sync with nature and full of deep insights. She has a keen ability to hear whispers of the natural world around her and always seems to be watching and listening.

Twice in our teenage years she wowed me. One evening we were driving down 78 West when the day began its surrender to the night. Gray waves were swooping over the blue of day, joining feathered strokes of orange and silver slashing softly across the sky. She was lost in a world of her own, but sensed me on the periphery and invited me in. "God is such a great artist," she said.

Her words raised my eyes from the mundane concrete of the highway and up into the wonder of the twilight skies. Although she was only seventeen, she had always been one who sensed Truth in the skies and was awed by it. Another time, while the house slept, I awoke in our dark bedroom to see my sister sitting on the edge of her bed. She was gazing in awe at the myriad of stars speckling the night sky. Her mouth was moving — she was praying in the white light of the moon. I needed her energy with me in pregnancy just as I needed her when we were younger.

We were not the bickering kind. We had endured greater things in the first decade of our lives together. The migration of our parents to America created an abyss that forced us to cling to each other. Five years later, we boarded the plane with a stranger and held each other's hands for the duration of the flight. We reunited with our parents in the vastness of LaGuardia Airport. We endured the biting cold of our first winter in a new country.

Growing up in New Jersey we shared a long narrow room. Our twin beds were positioned with not enough space between to fit our nightstand. We placed it at the foot of my bed, where it became home for our stereo. Music was the balm that healed and held us together in our teenage years. On weekdays, 106.7 Smooth Jazz and R&B lulled us to sleep. On Saturdays, the rhythms of an Indian CD caused our feet to move as we cleaned, polished, and swept. On Sunday evenings, for two hours between five and seven, Hot 97 with Bobby Konders and Jabba filled the airwaves with reggae. Sometimes, we turned the dial to 107.1 Real Country. While Reba sang stories about love and heartbreak and Rascal Flatts sang about broken roads, we closed our door and for hours created words on our worn Scrabble board. We were playing Scrabble the night I went into labor.

Chapter Ten

SUNSHINE STATE OF MIND

"I was a child in the world."

I left New Jersey in midwinter. The cold was hostile — forcing plants beneath the earth, sending animals into holes, and pushing sweet-chirping birds to the south. The sky had not been blue for months. The gray clouds blended into the snow, which had been plowed and side banked into mini hills — the peaks a wonder-white and roots a swirl of slushy charcoal. Although I was padded in layers — thermal leggings, earmuffs, and boots to the knees — I could still feel the sting of the cold. I searched for feelings in my fingers that were numb from pushing and pulling. With one hand I pushed the stroller carrying a cherubic baby atop and an overstuffed bag of diapers, wipes, and formula underneath. I pulled behind me a rolling suitcase firmly packed with our first week of clothing and toiletries.

When my bottom finally felt the cushion of the aircraft seat, I settled my daughter in my lap, and let my head lean into the headrest. I gazed through the window, a frosty magic tablet for children's tiny fingers to practice letters and drawings. There was grimness outside: baggage workers moved like drones, and planes arrived, refueled, and departed in a robotic fashion. Winter was suffocating. Come spring, the Garden State would burst forth a bed of green. I would not be there to see it. I was a child in the world now. I was pressing past the fear of leaving home and my family. I was embarking on finding myself.

Two-and-a-half hours later, the wheels of the aircraft cried out as they hit the tarmac at the Fort Myers airport. The warmth of the Florida sun pierced the window, soaked into the pores of my face, and massaged me — loosening my neck, my arms, and my entire body. I could feel the sun tiptoeing on the fringes of my mind, seeking to light the dark. I inhaled so deeply my exhale detected an unknown place within me. I had known the weight of my burdens: the Rastaman and his threats of taking me to court and forcing me to remain in New Jersey; the shame of being a black single mother; and moving into my mother's basement with my two-month-old baby.

I could not have known the ease of freedom. I became aware of my breath in Florida. I played with it often: inhaling and filling the well of my belly with free air, then slowly exhaling, pushing the air out like a slowly deflating balloon. The last several months had been anything but fun or free.

I had moved back home ashamed of failing and epitomizing my mother's justifiable fears: a daughter, unwed with a child. My mother graciously offered me my old room — the one I shared with my sister. I declined. It felt too open and welcoming. I needed to be secluded, within the confines of my own space to tend to my brokenness and hopefully heal. I moved into a room in the basement and created a mini Shangri-La for my daughter and me. I painted the walls white, fainting once when I unwisely closed the door and inhaled the fumes. I draped the window with a sheer curtain and hung a mirror opposite it to let in more light. I dismantled my twin bed, carried it piece by piece down the stairs, and screwed it back together. Beside my bed, I placed the secondhand crib I had purchased for fifty dollars. When my daughter and I were alone, I sang songs, read her stories, and basked in the light her energy had brought into my life. I was at peace behind our walls. I found refuge in my room in the basement.

Beyond the basement, two emotions vied for dominance on the faces of those with whom I came in contact. While lips offered encouraging smiles, eyes asked the mournful question, What now? People outside gazed at me with pity, as though my life had ended, but I was wobbling around, refusing to lie down and die. I had known the expectations: education, marriage, children. I also knew I had switched them, muddling the first and last together, shredding any real chance of marriage. With each inquiry from concerned family and friends hoping to guide me to a state of enlightenment, I felt more burdened and less hopeful. I double-dutched between panic and peace. The searching eyes outside of the basement envisioned the baby on my arm as the scarlet letter — the result of not acquiescing to abortion, encouraged by some

Holy Ghost-filled Christians in my circle. I could not survive the loudness of my silent critics, the judgments, and pretentious well-wishes. I was the plant beneath the snow, plowed and pushed aside, and suffocating. I retreated to the basement and tried to catch a breath by applying for jobs with the Irvington, New Jersey Board of Education.

I worked as a long-term substitute teacher at Washington Elementary, one of the toughest schools in Irvington. After thirty-seven years of serving as a music teacher, my predecessor had retired, leaving behind shoes that could not be filled by just anyone. She was a phenomenon, I was told. Students looked forward to her class. She was the reason many had reached the pinnacle of graduating from high school. Stepping into her classroom was like stepping into shoes three sizes too large and two inches too wide. It was my first job out of college. I was new, and a substitute. I couldn't fill a single one of her shoes, much less a pair of them. The students dared me to try.

A few minutes before the bell rang, I stood at the entrance of my classroom, prepared to greet each student with a warm welcome and a handshake. I stood with an outstretched arm in vain. Each of them, as though rehearsed, smirked, and inspected my hand as though it was infested with maggots. They were young, hard, and uncaring. I closed the door just after the late bell rang, signaling to the latecomers they would need a hall pass from the office.

I was standing in front of the class introducing myself when a young lady entered the room, looked me up and down, rolled her eyes, and sat down. No hall pass, and within three point five seconds she was already bored with my introduction. She stood, called the class to attention as though she was The Queen B, and like worker bees, they looked to her for guidance. When she had gained their attention and she knew it, she turned to me and X-rayed me once again: "Why don't you get your white-speaking ass outta here?" she asked. The class laughed. I wanted to burrow my way into the ground. I heard a dormant but bold voice expelled from within me. "Have a seat," the voice said. I was no longer my parents' child. I was a woman, the mother of a little girl, and a teacher in the making.

When I was replaced by a permanent music teacher a few days shy of my contracted time, I stood before the class just as I had done months earlier and told the class I was leaving. The young Queen B hung her head. When she lifted her face, her eyes were red from silently crying. She stayed after class and asked to speak with me. There was something familiar about our conversation — something in her face and demeanor that was not far from me. I knew without her saying so, but she confessed that she was pregnant. I left no longer hating her for making my first teaching experience so excruciatingly painful, but appreciating the confidence I had gained from my interactions with her. I thought about her often when I moved to the Sunshine State.

In my first home in Florida, there was a sense of

tranquility reminiscent of my room in my mother's basement. I did not know anyone, nor did I care to; I reveled
in the quietness. For three months, I did not have contact
with the outside world. My thoughts and moments were
not interrupted by the invasive dinging of a cell phone or
ringing of a landline. When I was ready to share pieces
of myself, I phoned my mother — about once a week —
from Sister Iris' phone.

She was my neighbor and an older Jamaican
woman who spoke of Judgment Day and The Rapture in
the same breath. On Saturdays she faithfully brought me
a bowl of beef soup and continued to do so even after I
got my own telephone for job callbacks. The phone ser-
vicemen came, desecrated my space with their dirty boots,
and inserted wires into the walls that would let the outside in. The first time the phone rang, I was reading Dr.
Seuss' Horton Hears a Who to my daughter. The ringing
was loud, disturbing my solitude — it alarmed and an-
noyed me. I jumped to my feet and yanked it out of the
wall.

I had fallen perhaps too deeply in love with the stillness and order of my days. In the mornings, the sun streamed through the trees, through my bedroom window, where it woke me to new possibilities. I took long showers before my daughter woke from her sleep. It was a splendid gift of time to enjoy relaxing my muscles and mind, and to find solace between body and spirit. I learned that warm water running over me was grace. Showers became a form of worship: I lathered myself with Oil of Olay and let healing memories run through my mind. I moisturized and soaked in encouraging thoughts along with the refreshing scent of the cream. I learned then to dress as though I was, in fact, going somewhere. I made breakfast, played with my daughter, looked through the classifieds, and made a few calls. Usually in the afternoons — about three — it rained.

If it was not thundering, my little girl and I danced in the rain and played in the puddles before the sun renewed itself and soaked it all up. At first, I carried my daughter in my arms on evening walks along the canal that ran beside our backyard. One day she wiggled her way out of my arms and stood on legs not yet strong, but determined. I watched as she stood and then fell flat on her rear end. She stood again, looked up at me, and took one step. She learned to walk not long after — steadying her feet, tumbling, falling, and getting back up on her wobbly legs. My daughter and I were both learning to walk that year — her on her feet, me on mine.

Chapter Eleven

THE REMARKABLES

*"The music of rain falling watered our
juvenile souls."*

I started teaching at The Marine Institute, a court-ordered program for juvenile delinquents, the day after my twenty-third birthday. Ontonio, my friend since birth, called from Jamaica to wish me a happy birthday. It was a great new day. I was hired as a full-time teacher at the school on Fort Myers Beach. I thought about the mediocre teachers I had had versus the three remarkable ones woven into the fabric of my academic life. With my new opportunity, I felt the urge, a hope, to be somewhat like them — Mr. Edwards during primary school, Mr. Bryant in high school, and Professor Sanchez in college. They each left behind droplets of wisdom at various stages in the ebb and flow of my life, each an oasis to sustain me in the desert of pedestrian teachers, who were plentiful.

Mr. Edwards was my fifth-grade teacher in Jamaica. His boyish face was airbrushed a deep chocolate, warm and melting. He wore both a sharp and gentle edge to his smile that awakened me to the pulsing of my heart — its ability to increase in frequency and volume in my ears. His presence sent an awareness throughout my entire body and left an unquenched desire behind the flatness of my pubescent left breast. He taught lessons of which he was unaware. When raindrops morphed into a downpour, he honored it. He too became a student; he paused his lesson. At the gesture of his neatly kept chin, a student sitting in close proximity to the light switch would turn it off. Another would open the door and windows. We knew it was time to rest our heads on our desks and keep our thoughts in our heads. The music of rain falling watered our juvenile souls. In the afternoons when the earth had stopped its tears, our ritual was simple. We lined up and walked beside him, our uniforms marking us as his — full suit khaki pants for the boys, the hues of blue dresses tickling girls' knees. We sat beneath the shade of a tree rustled by the breeze. A book in his hand, he would read to us the flowing words of poetry. Each word he said seemed to linger on the melodies of men whistling in the fields below. My fifth-grade soundtrack: words, whistling, whispering of trees.

Mr. Bryant at Orange High School in New Jersey

was a true comedic genius turned high school social science teacher. He was a rotund man, unpleasant in physical features, with large bulging, protruding eyes. He had not been pleasurable to look at, but there were rich and varied layers beyond his flesh. He often taught without books, telling stories of which the Board of Education would disapprove but would turn their heads once they saw our test scores. I never had to study difficult political terms such as pump-priming for his exams. "Pump-priming," he would say, his large eyes expanding for emphasis and his eyebrows raising and lowering as in a dance, "is when boys, like politicians, know they have to put something in to get something out...watch out, girls, they don't carry your books and bags for nothing." His stories are all stored in my memory. Alongside the image of his face there is the sound of his laughter, the image of his hands slapping his knees, his jiggling belly hanging over his crotch as he laughed at his own hilarity.

Professor Sanchez stepped onto the stage of my college education with grace. He was dressed almost flamboyantly — his shirt tucked in, and a cloth belt around his waist holding his pants a tad too high.

Before Professor Sanchez, I was a student at Caldwell College, a Catholic operation run by nuns. A few of them lived in Rosary Hall, an all-girls dormitory to which I had been assigned. Other nuns were dead and buried just outside my dorm room window, the only window that let light into the already dark space of my life. The thought of me putting a shoelace around my neck scared the shit out of me. It was the first time I had thought maybe I didn't belong in college or even in this world. I sought counseling with the Sisters, then pleaded with my mother for a transfer to Kean University.

I was in my second semester at Kean when the sense of non-belonging resurfaced. I was sitting in a Communication 101 class taught by Professor Cameron, a middle-aged man who — at a rushed glance of the syllabus — had filled the academic quarter with videos of Britney Spears. She was singing "Baby One More Time" upon our entrance, and he played another song after his introduction. He was smitten by her. I was confused. I got up and moved towards the front of the class, unaware of what I would do. When the class paused, he looked over at me quizzically. It was then I tossed the syllabus onto his desk, then looked at him and said, "If this is what you're teaching, I want no part of it." I walked out the door into a scary blank space.

I found a corner in which I would confide my fears, expressed in tears. A soft voice asked if I wanted to talk about it. It was Professor Sanchez who listened to me, snot and all, and proceeded to remind me of the introduction to sociology class I had taken with him during my first summer. I remembered. I belonged in his class. Education seemed attainable, dare I say enjoyable. He had walked in, books on his hip, his other hand in the air, his voice raised in great enthusiasm, and with an underlying chuckle he exclaimed: "Class, today we are going to study dead white men." If only all my classes could be this way, college would indeed be for me. However, prerequisites had to be fulfilled, each of them a heaping of dirt poured onto the coffin, covering the light and freedom I'd felt the summer prior. With his slight reminder, I signed up for another one of his classes: Personal and Social Interaction. I was hooked. His classes became the place where I found pieces of myself. I came to know that because he listened to me and challenged me to create my own perspectives.

He was disciplined, and he ran a strict classroom with an extremely selective vocabulary. For an entire semester he stopped all frivolous conversations by exclaiming "BS!" This was a prominent declaration, urging us to put an immediate end to inauthentic conversations that reeked of flatulence. He did not stand for the how's-the-weather type conversation; rather, he provoked us intellectually by calling us outside our preconceived thoughts and premature beliefs. It was in one of his classes, after he gave a tear-jerking lecture about immigrants and farmworkers, I gleaned that knowledge could not be stuffed into brains like nuts into chipmunk cheeks. Learning was not separate from Life. His lecture stirred memories of my father.

My father had died, completing his circle in my life, but that semester he came alive again in my memories: good ones and hard ones — his offenses against me and lessons he taught me. He had been a strong believer in having friends from all walks of life. "Even a thief can be a good friend," he said. And in the same breath he would also remind us, "Your siblings are your friends; you don't need any more friends... and for chrissakes, stay away from African-Americans! They are angry." This warning of anger was coming from the same man who, when I told him about being bullied at school, lost his mind. The first day at my American elementary school, I was served sloppy joes for lunch. When the meat splashed onto my tray, I could barely hold the gag and what proceeded from my mouth. After that, I didn't eat school lunches; lunchtime for me was a time to rest. To avoid the mockeries of being the weirdo not eating, or to be called chocolate or banana boat, I crossed my hands on the table, put my head in the cave of my arms, and pretended I was taking a nap. I had gone unnoticed until a lad, fresh from an alternative learning center, took a liking to my back and decided to make it his lounge chair. I moved. He followed.

When I told my father the reason for my long face one evening over dinner, it would change the trajectory of our lives at school, and on our block. Literally. The next day, with a machete in his firm left hand, fueled with anger, he barged through the chained school doors. He moved briskly past the sign-in sheet at the security desk and went straight to the intercom in the main office. "This is Kadine, Monalisa, and Lasana's father. If any of you shitheads ever touch a strand of hair on their heads, I will..." The announcement, although brief, had guaranteed our remaining two years at my elementary would be without incident. No one spoke to us with indifference. Children graduated with the memory; new students were told the story of the man with a heavy accent who entered their school and scared them shitless. I was a proud child of the crazy Jamaican.

My father himself had African-American friends and love interests, so his earlier advice stood on a slippery slope. It was in college, however, in Professor Sanchez's class, that I learned firsthand the wrath of raw anger — not from all African-Americans, but from one specific young lady, Tatiana. The class was diverse in culture, but unlike what we had been taught about finding the similarities amongst us, Professor Sanchez placed our differences of race, ethnicity, and religious beliefs on the table — like a grandiose American Thanksgiving dinner. It was teeth-gritting and uncomfortable. He asked questions like, "What about my Cuban presence upsets you?" He asked questions whose answers were often shared in a hushed tone, within secret corners, and with trusted confidants. It was real and intense. Most times we sat in suffocating silence.

I was telling a story in class about the challenges of growing up in Jamaica — walking to school for an hour in the rain or hot sun. If we were late, we were beaten with sticks that should have been used to start a fire but instead sparked our backsides. Like one possessed, Tatiana growled from her gut: "Shut the fuck up, Kadine... at least you have a culture! All we have is collard greens and macaroni and cheese." She was inflamed with anger so strong I thought she had flown from behind her desk and lashed me with her hands, clawing my face with her outgrown nails instead of her words. Her anger was not rooted in the foods, it was deeper. Her wailing told me so. I tried processing her anger through my own experiences and found it an impossibility. Not having been raised in America, I had been unable to place the depth of her pain.

Chapter Twelve

FALSE NICE

*"They spoke and we sat in what felt
like a bath of acid."*

The words of my father and the image of Tatiana's enraged face became my false defense, the justifiable reasons to keep my distance from African-Americans. Words and images had become my crutch, working perfectly and without a glitch until I met Marquita — the woman who would teach me the meaning of friendship. With the exception of an Indian anchor at Wink News in Fort Myers, Marquita and I were the only "melanoid" women amid eighty-plus white women at MOPS — Mothers of Preschoolers Support.

I arrived at MOPS seeming well on the outside but was inwardly battling postpartum depression after having my son. I declined the medication offered to me by my doctor and instead took my husband's advice to attend the support group at the church. MOPS was akin to licking honey from thorns, hurting and healing served on the same silver platter. There were savory and sweet foods, homemade breakfast casseroles, fruits, pastries, coffee, and tea — foods to feed the physical hunger within us.

As for our inner being, there were speakers, usually mothers who were experiencing the complexities of motherhood. Some had carried babies within them for months, felt their kicks, and yet, in the end, given birth to a child without breath. Others were on their first or fifth miscarriage, while some were raising a child with special needs. Other mothers brought balance by sharing the simple and comedic side of parenting. As each shared her own colorful shade of motherhood, it pushed us back to the center of our own stories, struggles, and successes. There were also weekly crafts — like the gratitude jar — and projects I could take home and share with my growing family. Then there were the table mothers. They were women who had already raised their children and many were even grandmothers. Jan was a table mother and had recently returned from living in Colombia. The air of arrogance and privilege had been erased and replaced with an air of grace. She and Marquita were a balm to the woman and mother in me searching for the light turned off by postpartum depression.

Marquita and I were the Ones: the One black woman with the One black family showing up at events to which a verbal welcome did not match the undertone. Marquita and I drove in from Lehigh Acres, through the invisible line of economic barbed wire, to arrive in Fort Myers. The shock of it all felt like a sting to the back. We sat with women who rode on the esteem of both their possessions and husbands' professions — the lawyers, the doctors. They spoke in the most humble manner about their benevolence — how they volunteered with the poor black children, packed shoeboxes with white dolls for children in Haiti at Christmas. This great kindness was inspired by the same video played in previous years about poor black children in far-off lands, the same fly buzzing on the lips of the same malnourished boy. There was pity for the poor black souls — and a brief burden was eased by their volunteering and packing. They spoke and Marquita and I sat in what felt like a bath of acid. We often held each other's gaze as a means of comfort — our eyes locked, communicating a space of understanding and home.

Marquita had introduced herself to me one day after our MOPS meeting. I did the false-nice greeting, customary to the assimilation process of the '90s, with "Hi. How are you?" slipping off my tongue but not caring about the response buried beneath the custom. Marquita actually meant it when she asked, "How are you?" It took some time for me to recognize it. She was patient. We exchanged numbers. She called. I listened. We spoke on the phone casually for a few weeks. Then one morning while I was home doing my mommy routine — a timed twenty minutes of putting everything in place and running the vacuum — my doorbell rang.

While I do not remember giving her my address, it is with certainty that I say it is stored in Marquita's mind like the birth date of a child. She is meticulous, has a knack for details, and the memory of an elephant. For the next two years, after she dropped her four older children off at school in the mornings, she arrived at my house with her son, who was just a few weeks older than my little fellow. The boys played with blocks and trains. Marquita and I unfolded ourselves through conversations. We talked, ate crackers and cheese, drank flavored tea: scalding hot tea straight out of the kettle for me, and an ice cube or two in her Lemon Zinger.

We did things differently. She watched in amazement as I cooked oatmeal from scratch for my son's breakfast — boiling water in the pot, adding oatmeal, a pinch of salt, brown sugar, condensed milk, cinnamon, and nutmeg. I frowned when she pulled out an instant pack of oatmeal, added water, and placed it in the microwave. At first, she did not say anything about my wide-eyed responses. But one day she said my name with an edge I had not heard before. I stopped. The space between us and the concern on her face caused a breaking inside of me, akin to a shovel splitting a patch of earth. "You're judgmental," she said.

Perhaps I learned too well from my mother's skill with malice, but I guarded myself by keeping the sound of my words from Marquita. I did not accept her calls for a few days, but she called still. When I finally answered one of her calls, she made it clear she was not apologizing for what she said. She was, however, apologizing for her tone. She had been told before, her tone had a bite. During my time of withdrawal, I had come to learn that she was right. I was an uptight Jamaican with ethnocentric mannerisms. She had seen me riding into our friendship fully armored, my head held high, my rear end saddled on my majestic black horse. She decided her course: dismount me from my horse with her words, then hold my hand as I walked among the plebeians, each of us with our own handicaps.

Whether hers was an actual handicap or not, Marquita once described herself as a shot of whiskey: it burns at first, a head shake follows, but then it warms you up on the inside. I had already learned this was true, but I also learned she was sensitive, vigilant, and brave. She must have learned the art of friendship, forgiveness, and loving the broken from Jesus Christ himself. On various occasions, I watched her interact with others and cringed at the behaviors she accepted from them. For one of her monthly Mom's Night Out events with a few ladies from her church, she invited me and I accepted. We had not been at the get-together long before Marquita excused herself to the restroom. At the turn of her back, a blonde's eyes did their orbit. She was the young lady Marquita introduced me to as a close friend, and she was the first to whisper to the others about Marquita in her absence. Some chuckled while the others shook their heads. I knew it was the first and the last time I would accept an invitation to spend time with those ladies.

When I asked Marquita how she was able to endure it all, she said, verbatim: "They each offer something different and valuable outside the context of this group. I value them for the richness they offer to my life and forgive them for the ways in which they mistreat me in my absence. I forgive them because they just don't know better." Forgiveness was a hard concept for me to understand. I found Marquita's ability to forgive with such ease either a character flaw or a great strength.

Marquita's mother was absent during her childhood. She was raised mostly by her older brothers and sisters. This lack of motherly guidance may have contributed to her being who she was, becoming a mother at such a young age. She used her mother's absence as motivation to be an exceptionally present mother herself. When people gawked at her in disbelief, exclaiming in surprise how demanding it must be to have five children, she responded with grace. "Yes. I have been blessed to have five rivers flowing from and into me." Her nuggets were rooted in the wisdom of everyday life, and she shared with me enough to embed them in my psyche. She shared, "Window shopping requires patience, but you get to know the pieces you love over time — the way it fits, the way it feels — and then you wait for the price to drop." Marquita perused each item carefully before any decision was made, sometimes for months at a time.

She gave me compliments on my girls' clothing and advised on my son's. She had three boys and I had a very young one, so she had more experience. When it came to socks, she shared much-needed advice: ankle socks are for summer days and sneakers, thin ones are for dress shoes, thick mid-calf or above are for winter boots. For those pesky little feet that kicked the back of her seat while she drove, she carried a silicone spatula with a wooden handle. It was her final threat against their kicking feet, which usually worked, eliminating the need for further action. "Our hands, when raised, should never make our children cower, but invite them to open up like budding flowers."

The first time Marquita said her ovaries sometimes hurt, I brushed it off as her just being super sensitive. At the time, I was experiencing terrible pelvic pain — a cycle twice a month laying me flat on my bed in a dark room for two days. I ignored all incoming phone calls, but there were days I could hear her gently opening my bedroom door and joining me in the dark silence. She brought canned soup, which I could not bring myself to open, and Midol for pain relief. When I was out in the light again, she was adamant. "You have built up an extremely high tolerance for pain. The agony you're experiencing is not normal; you are not okay." I had not had a friend who cared so genuinely for me when I was so vulnerable.

As the time came for my family to move from Florida to Atlanta, Marquita helped me pack with a heavy heart but ready hands. She did make it clear, however, that my moving was taking a piece of her. I felt it too. Our two years' worth of conversations had created roots and branches strong enough for me to inspect and discuss my father's advice and Tatiana's angry words. Marquita agreed with them. After all, in the African-American community, there is some anger for the pain endured and the injustices that continue. But I learned from Marquita we are all layered and textured people.

When we grew tired from packing, Marquita lay on my bed, like a sister, and offered thoughts on the area I struggled with the most: "Friends don't come complete. Each person has something to teach and something to learn; give people a chance, and they might surprise you."

After I moved, I often thought about Marquita, and when I called to say I was thinking about her, she would pause, and say "Thank you." She often mused, "Thoughts and hearts are sacred spaces. To be a part of them is to be stored in one's mental treasure box."

Chapter Thirteen

THE VILLAGE

*"Sometimes we altered between
laughter and lamentations."*

The Village was the name of our community at Columbia Theological Seminary in Atlanta. It was designated for seminarians with spouses and children — a tender approach telling us to keep our cute and crazy family stuff off campus, away from the single students and the academic buildings. The Village was compact — possessing only four buildings, each housing six apartments. In front of each building, a chipped red bench was strategically placed facing the playground. It was crafted in the center of a mound, a seemingly sacred space that drew our children to play every day. Parents gathered on their respective benches in the afternoons like medics on duty while children frolicked on swings, glided down slides, and built imaginary worlds in sandboxes.

The fullness of life happening in the Village beneath a canopy of trees was inconspicuous to passersby. They walked past our complex with their dogs and drove by in their cars unaware that people uprooted their lives, left families and friends behind, came long distances to arrive at this campus for three years of intense theological study. The Village was in and of itself a reclusive society filled with its own life experiences that spanned the spectrum between awe and bitterness. It contained a variety of conflicting ideologies brought by conservative and liberal Presbyterians, a few non-denominationalists, a lone Baptist, and one or two African-American Methodists. At times they wove themselves into something akin to a baby's blanket — soft, warm, and protective. Their new, deepened perspective was a source of awe. Other times, they knitted themselves into something like a coarse burlap bag, refusing to loosen the ties on long-held ideas. For three years we moved between awe and irritation, negotiating the complications and connectivity of living in the Village.

Summer in the Village was the season of hard goodbyes to those who were moving off campus to pastor or to start a ministry dear to their hearts. It was also a time of saying hearty hellos to newcomers who would maneuver their way into a community that was forever changing. When it was our turn at newness, I met Gretchen — four months pregnant with Amos — at one of the Spouses of Seminarians gatherings. We shared a few details about ourselves, and a few days later she with her two boys knocked on our door. The three came bearing a welcome goodie bag — sturdy plastic cups and plates, S'more wire for Friday night cookouts. She also had a birthday gift for my little guy who would be turning three in four days. I was in a new state, in a new home, at the beginning of a wonderful new friendship.

On campus, seminarians studied in groups or in solitude, vented about professors and their teaching styles, and griped about their love/hate relationship with buying and reading so many books. They studied Greek and Hebrew, read and dissected heart-wrenching bible stories — like the cry of Tamar — that affected their psyches for days on end. They went out on internships, becoming men and women of the cloth through church ministry, and providing care for the sick, the mourners, and the dying through chaplaincy. Spouses listened, encouraged, bandaged boo-boos, fed the family, cleaned the house, edited papers, did the laundry, and wiped the same floor of the twentieth spill. Tired from the week's saga, the community gathered on blankets and at tables to share a communal cookout on Friday nights. Diverse families — Americans, Koreans, Jamaicans — brought meat for the grill and a side to share. The varieties of food ranged from Korean barbecue, bulgogi, and a crawfish boil to curry chicken and dumplings, brown-sugared bacon, and home-brewed beer. Adults fed their children, then when the sun submitted to the moon, sent them off to play sharks and minnows, hide and seek, and night tag. Parents with younger children left early for BBB — bath, book, and bed. Others lingered behind to declutter their minds, listen to music, talk themselves into new or deeper friendships. Sometimes we altered between laughter and lamentations.

Cloistered though it was, the Village life had its joy but did not escape deviations in quality any more than life in the world did. The aberrations just felt, perhaps, a bit more concentrated, more stinging because of the compactness of the seminary complex. In our time there, we shared the shock, the questioning, the underpinning support for a young marriage shattered because of a husband's unfaithfulness, leaving his spouse bitter and broken. There was no time to heal. Just time to focus on a toddler — to bathe, feed, and potty train.

A year into our seminary journey, another couple — Ed and Sue, who had married later in life — joyously shared news of their pregnancy. Just as Sue's belly began showing, throat cancer crept into Ed's vivacious body. For months they fought cancer and cravings. When she gave birth to their beautiful red-headed boy, it was without the support of her husband, who was quarantined on another floor of the hospital. His weakened red blood cells put his life in grave jeopardy. After missing an entire semester of classes, Ed fought hard to make up the credits and graduate with the men and women with whom he'd started his seminary journey. When his name was called at graduation, those of us who had listened to the play-by-play of doctor's visits and updates knew we were witnessing a miracle. People stood, applauded, and cried in concert with Ed's achievement.

In another vein, flesh-eating bacteria claimed a pregnant mother's hands, feet, and a fetus that should have been a younger sibling. Even the seminary's president was not immune to disappointment in the quest to maintain quality of life. He once spoke with grace at welcoming events and graduations, but for months we knew his kidneys were failing and he was dying. Then one day, his spirit rose like heat in summer, leaving his body to grow cold, his spouse and children thrashing in sorrow. Life in the Village continued — breaking, building again, and demanding we share ourselves. It was then that we learned to BE a community, lest we one day become the ones in need.

Our joy emerged from sharing. Children full of youth and life gathered sticks — the older ones challenging themselves by hauling large logs from behind our apartment, in preparation for respite. Our neighbor taught us the art of building a long-lasting fire by making a teepee out of the wood. We sat around the fire pit when the day passed and twilight embedded itself in the night. We watched the fire spark and sing in orange flame.

A friend came by every Wednesday morning to teach my children Russian. She brought them a sample of her favorite tea and they made Russian sandwiches — one slice of bread instead of two, with a topping of choice. She shared with them her favorite Russian cartoon from when she was growing up.

Our Korean neighbors shared their language, food, and customs. I became an honorary young sister to Korean women who embraced their roles of being older with pride. I had an enlightening conversation about the map on their living room wall where Asia was placed at the center. When our neighbors were sick, we alternated making and receiving dinners from meal trains. A spicy chili and sweet cornbread remains my favorite.

We hosted reading time and movie nights at our home and watched children without a common language play to their hearts' content. Young adults — often viewed as selfish — wholeheartedly played with younger children on the playground or offered to babysit.

We expanded our understanding of faith as we learned from each other that God shows up differently in each of our stories. God became greater than the narrow-minded, self-serving images we carried in our heads. We learned that God is neither male nor female, but in fact deeper, larger than we had initially thought. The beauty of life together is that we learned building and breaking, healing and growing gives us the power to be loving, resilient beings.

Chapter Fourteen

A CUP OF TEA

"Her thoughts and abilities would forever be split in two: between before and after."

John, ShanAe, and their two-year-old son, Kevin, lived in Apartment 2, three doors down from us in Apartment 6. John, in his final year of seminary, was anticipating graduation, and accepting his first call as a pastor. ShanAe was a stay-home mother. In the cold winter months and hot summer days she entertained Kevin on their soft, multicolored carpet tiles. On days when the temperature had manners, ShanAe and Kevin joined my kids and me outside. She and I sat on the bench and danced in and out of conversations as we watched and listened to our children play.

On Thursday evenings, she attended an English class at the library. While it was helpful, she confided in me that her struggle was not with reading or writing, it was comprehending English in conversation. We were a mosaic of mother tongues and second languages. My Jamaican accent rested in my bosom, except for with family, when sometimes it slipped out with some h and th words — appy for happy, teet for teeth. ShanAe's Korean remained a dominatrix to her English — some words left her mouth with diced syllables. She asked if I would correct her grammar and when I did, would I speak to her slowly. English speakers, she said, had a way of racing through their words, and she needed to take note of the movement of my lips and the placement of my tongue. I chortled at the idea of teaching her English for two reasons: she knew more English than her Korean counterparts, and I never paid attention to the position of my English tongue, which was my second language.

When an African-American student's car was sprayed with the N-word, it shocked many and led to a gathering of the minority seminarians on campus. My husband and I hosted the group in our home for breakfast. I made an Italian cranberry cornmeal cake and gluten-free almond cake. I placed them on our long farmhouse table along with an array of cups for flavored tea or coffee made with condensed milk. It was a good meeting that revealed a number of ideas to explore. After the meeting, John shared the great news: ShanAe was pregnant with their second child. They had waited until she entered her second trimester when, according to their culture, it was safe to share their merriment. ShanAe's pregnancy would join the promises of their new beginnings in the spring. Congratulations and well wishes traveled quickly to their door.

ShanAe seemed a little tired, but nothing out of the ordinary for being pregnant. She seemed her usual soft-spoken self — grateful and gracious. When I did not see her outside for a few weeks, I reserved my questions. I assumed her absence from the bench was a result of pregnancy zapping her energy.

Panic, then relief, then dread would haunt the Village over the next three months. It was just before bedtime when an ambulance sped onto the concrete and the siren penetrated the brick walls of our apartments. The siren rushed its way into our community and left just as quickly, like the sound of a fetus' first heartbeat. The distance swallowed the sound. The night went still, and only at the break of morning did we learn that tragedy had rampaged through John and ShanAe's home.

We heard updates only in bits and pieces. While many rested in the blissfulness of sleep, ShanAe was rushed into surgery, where she fought for her life the entire night. John leaned on the words of nurses and doctors, and little Kevin slept in a Village bed that was not his own. No one wanted to intrude, but everyone was eager to hear whatever update came via the persons who sat with John at Northside Hospital. My husband was a chaplain at the hospital during this time. He regularly sought out updates, but things were happening so fast that by the time the news reached them, it had become history. Each new problem strived to outdo its antecedent. ShanAe was fighting for her life between high fevers, surgeries, coma, and life support. John lived in the hospital. He came home for showers, and sometimes slept if he could. He would visit with his son, who was living with neighbors. Women stood outside each other's door, held hands, and prayed for healing. We all waited, and searched through whatever information we gleaned for hints as to what was really happening. I learned waiting is like being hung to dry in the scorching sun — arms up and pinched with clothespins, forgotten and growing crisp. We grew thirsty, wanting to know more, waiting for answers, wanting to lift our hands to help.

The events followed like a blunt force object battering the same wound over and over again, its power undiminished. One night around seven-thirty, just after children were washed clean of the day's play and tucked into bed, the message that ShanAe had lost the baby was shared in broken whispers. It draped our hopes in darkness.

Next, we heard she was in a coma and had been placed on life support. John would have to make the decision whether or not to pull the plug. Life support? Pull the plug? It all sounded so far out of my understanding. The idea of pulling the plug had been like grasping air. When I heard the doctors had recommended her parents fly in from Korea to say their goodbyes, my feet felt mired in hardening concrete.

Emotionally shattered, a few of us managed to prepare John and ShanAe's apartment for her parents' arrival. The Korean women gathered and dispersed assignments. Women swept and mopped floors, changed the sheets, and made beds. Some purchased toiletries; others went grocery shopping and stocked the pantry with food and baskets with fruits. I washed and folded laundry.

Only through God's grace were we not overcome by the heaviness in the atmosphere of our little Village. The experience of having known, conversed, and laughed with someone on the verge of death gyrated mockingly over our heads. We all coaxed each other into having hope for John, who would lose his wife and become a single father. Kevin would lose his mother and we would lose a friend. We searched for words to cover the magnitude of such loss. Nothing we could do would bring relief.

ShanAe was out of her coma. The good news arrived when a Korean neighbor, who had gone to sit with John, knocked on my door. Unlike bad news that made us hold our bellies with our arms tied at the elbows, we hugged each other, trusting our heartfelt prayers had been heard. Breathing came easier, and we were no longer akin to a stiff piece of wood — rigid with fear of impending grief.

We celebrated only briefly. The news that her fever was rising curled its infested nails around our necks. The fever did not allow her body to fight off the infection that was rapidly growing and eating away her flesh. She was again in and out of a coma like revolving doors — coming into the light for a few hours and retreating into unconsciousness for days on end. With each rise in temperature, ShanAe lost a body part. The doctors debated, but eventually amputated one of her legs. The thought of ShanAe with one leg settled better than the thought of losing her completely. Gratitude was evident but was tested when her other leg was amputated a few days later. Her two legs were severed to save her life.

Minds could not make sense of the speed with which the bad news rolled over us, not giving us a moment to recoup. We had not yet assimilated to the news of the leg amputations before we learned they had to amputate her arms, one and then the other, from her elbows down. In less than two weeks, ShanAe lost her legs, her arms, and a baby growing inside of her. ShanAe's life was forever changed before she was even conscious of it. I thought about her coming home to clothing and shoes in her closet. I pictured her being alone in front of a mirror for the first time in three months. I imagined the moment she realized she could no longer dress herself without thinking of the days when she had feet and arms. She once had feet that ran towards her son, danced with her husband, and carried her wherever she desired with the slightest of thought. Just a few months prior ShanAe and I had sat on the chipped red bench watching our children play. Her only struggle then was learning English. Her struggle would now redefine her life — her marriage, her motherhood, and her place in the human family. Her thoughts and abilities would forever be split in two: between before and after.

ShanAe spent three turbulent months at Northside Hospital before she was released and returned home, changed. The Village prepared for her homecoming. Men pooled their resources and talents and built a wheelchair ramp at John and ShanAe's apartment. Someone made a Welcome Home banner, children blew up and tied balloons, a friend snipped wildflowers, and we placed it all on their front porch. I made a wreath and hung it on their door. A few weeks after ShanAe came home, I tried visiting, but the physical and emotional adjustments had worn her bare. I sent an invitation to John and ShanAe for a cup of tea, when she was ready. ShanAe sent her acceptance via voice text.

The morning they visited, I watched them from my window. John's gait was slow and steady, matching the mechanical steps of ShanAe's new prosthetic legs. John's arm looped under her arm — cut off at her elbow — forming a pretzel. Kevin walked behind them. When they finally reached a reasonable distance from our apartment, my husband and I stepped outside. We welcomed them in, and watched as they talked their way through her sitting on the couch. I was a perfect marinade of fear and awe. When I invited them to tea, I had not thought about all the practical challenges, the simple things like sitting. Amputation had been a word, disjointed and lingering in my head without an actual image to connect it to reality. I did not realize how insensitive my good intentions must have seemed. I feared saying or doing something offensive.

I sat with John and ShanAe while my husband made tea. He brought two cups out, one for ShanAe and one for me. He paused and battled internally: how does one with no arms drink a cup of tea? John thought it would be best to sit at the dining table. He helped ShanAe to the table, and she shimmied herself for a few minutes to get comfortable. The memory muscles in my arm began to do what was organic without a thought. I reached out, picked up my cup, pulled it up to my nose, and breathed in the aromatics of mint and ginger. ShanAe's cup remained untouched. Guilt and uncertainty gushed through me. I could sense her mentally mapping out her next move. I asked if I could help her and, without thought and with such celestial grace, she accepted.

For the next hour and a half, we took turns talking and listening to each other. I took a sip from my cup, rested it on the table, picked up her cup, and put it to her lips. She sipped. I sipped. We drank until our cups were empty but our hearts were full.

Chapter Fifteen

LIVE LIKE AN INTERIM

*"He flipped the page in his mind and
took us to the streets with which he
was so familiar."*

I met Robert one spring morning when I walked over to the Clothes Closet, a thrift store of sorts offering free clothing and household items to missionaries and seminarians. Our meeting morphed into introducing each other to our spouses. Robert and my husband met for coffee to discuss church, art, and photography. Yulia, his wife, and I went out for wine and thinly sliced fried potatoes at Thinking Man Tavern in Atlanta. One evening, my husband and I hosted them for dinner. I made Jamaican jerk ribs and string bean salad — beans cooked for five minutes, shocked with cold water, drizzled with virgin olive oil, and topped with dried cranberries and sunflower seeds. Yulia prepared a Russian salad, which was more like layers of textured mayonnaise. There were white layers of regular, whipped, and pulsed mayonnaise, topped with pomegranate seeds and sprigs of fennel. I tasted it and made every effort to refrain from contorting my face, but I failed. She laughed. Her mayonnaise salad untouched, she told me I didn't have to eat it. Russians love mayo, she said; they eat it with everything. She was not kidding! One of her favorite meals was spaghetti and mayo!

Yulia was tart and intriguing. She did not wear a bra to dinner that night, and the thin fabric of her shirt revealed the firmness of her breasts and the peaks of her nipples. She was raw and controversial and grateful to be in the United States. She appreciated the warmth of American greetings, but she did not easily buy into the western way of life. She was not pretentious — she said what she meant. Jokes that were culturally exclusive left her out of the belly laugh, but not for long. She remained unmoved, utterly blank in the face. At the simmering of laughter, she asked us politely for clarification. When and only if she understood the joke, she laughed. Hysterically. Alone. If she did not grasp the humor, she pouted her lips and shrugged her shoulders. She was as open to her new life in America as Robert was to ministry appointments.

We ate and sipped wine for over four hours, and as the night unfolded, we waded through each other's lives via memories and stories. Robert was an older gentleman — previously married, with grown children. Yulia might have been drawn to the security and distinction some older men exude. He certainly had both. However, they had one major area that differed. Yulia was a proclaimed atheist and Robert was a Christian, a pastor, and founder of This Child Here — an organization birthed from Robert's passion to serve the street kids in Ukraine.

My husband uncorked the second bottle of wine, while Robert flipped through the album in his mind. He guided us through the painful collapse of Ukraine's economic and social systems, after the fall of the Soviet Union. Government, banks, hospitals, schools, houses, and social services crumbled. Adults turned to vodka; children ran away from physical and sexual abuse. He took us to the streets with which he was so familiar. He explained it was not uncommon to see children pressing their chests to the ground and crawling through a small opening in an abandoned building. The only light was from a candle in someone's hand. Once inside, they crawled over used cups and old clothes dotting the space until they reached their underground home. They joined other undernourished children lying on newspaper beds, a doll sitting off to the side. Their breaths reeked of glue from empty bottles scattered about, the fumes already inhaled into their lungs. They shared a bag of sunflower seeds and crackers. On the concrete wall, there was a childlike drawing of a house with smoke coming out of the chimney.

Robert took photographs of the children and showed them in galleries around Italy, hoping to raise awareness and funds to support the street kids. He brought a few photographs from Italy and had them in the church office where he was the interim pastor. A few weeks later, I scanned through the photographs in his office, pausing and connecting faces to Robert's words over dinner. One photograph struck me in the belly. In it, a group of children are blurred in the background, the focus instead on a little boy no older than twelve. He was resting on someone's leg, and a needle filled with drugs protruded from a vein in his neck. Robert told us they had made the drugs from boiling ephedrine, vinegar, and potassium permanganate. Within months, the children exposed to this drug lose their motor skills; their ability to pick things up or even to walk. They are locked up in their minds with no connection to their physical bodies.

Perplexed both by the picture and at the thought of Robert just standing behind the lens of his camera, I silently damned him. How could he take such horrific shots? Up close? Condemnation in my voice, I asked him how he, as an adult, a father — a pastor, for crying out loud — could just stand behind the lens of his camera and watch children insert drugs into their bodies. His answer altered my perspective. First he explained that the street children do not trust adults, so he had to earn their trust before he could make a difference in their behavior. Running in and grabbing the needle would do nothing but make him an enemy.

Street kids were neglected and abandoned, and most had been on their own for as long as they could remember. They only trust each other. There are children as young as four years old under the care of teenagers. When the weather gets below zero, they find each other and go under the railroad tracks or deep into caves.

Robert went on to tell us he hoped he had made progress by forming relationships with them. He felt that taking pictures was a way to draw closer to them, and make them permanent in the vision of those who saw the photos. This was a way to raise funds to help the street kids.

"When I go searching for them," he said, "they know I am not a threat. I am coming to feed them, replacing tight shoes and clothing, offering blankets to keep them warm, and listening with a non-judgmental ear."

Robert's understanding of his role suddenly made it clear to me: we are all interims. Wherever we find ourselves, we use it as a base. Sometimes a year, sometimes more. In our time, we accept and we give, filling in the gaps we see around us. To say we will be in one place forever — to promise to stay — is to say we won't live or shift with the tide, and that would be disturbingly impru-dent. We are called to seasons, just as we are called out from them. The insight poured out of him like oil, and my soul recognized it as truth because it entered and struck me like a match against flint, sparking at first and then engulfing me with a new light. Living like an interim is understanding that our time is limited, measured in mo-ments, each one sacred in its unfolding. Robert became a fast friend, maybe because we knew the time and space we shared would be brief.

Chapter Sixteen

TOY BOX

"No reason is justifiable to teach hate."

Seminary was an academic journey for my husband, but the course I found myself taking was an emotional one. My actual unwinding began when I audited a class entitled Externally Focused Church. Dr. Watts, in one of his lectures began, "Racism begins in your child's toy box." His words were like high-voltage electricity sprinting through me, jolting me awake, and forcing me to mentally scan through my children's toy box. I knew I would not find a diverse array of dolls there because I had chosen black. As a young mother, I was adamant at first that my girls receive only educational toys as gifts — and no dolls. I preferred puzzles of all shapes and sizes.

My stance against dolls had changed only a few years earlier because a mother, whom I admired, asked if she could pass on one of her daughter's favorite dolls to my girls. I blatantly told her it was okay as long as it was a brown doll with kinky and tightly curled hair to match that of my daughters. No long brunette or blonde hair lingering on the doll's back. I told her I wanted my girls to know that grooming our hair was not simply achieved in mere minutes with a few strokes of a brush. The doll offered by this friend met my criteria, and it became my girls' first doll. They shared.

As Dr. Watts' lecture went on, I felt my temperament rise, spiking between uncomfortable and defensive. My reasons for not giving my girls white dolls were justifiable, I thought. Images of my children were not represented in the media, not in the princess books that overflowed the library shelves, nor in magazines on the checkout aisles. An image of a super-heroine brown girl was not readily available. So it was with a tremendous amount of intention that I gathered a few books — mostly biographies — with characters who represented them. When there were no images, but I loved the message of a particular book, I created diversified characters with colored pencils.

As though he knew what I was thinking, Dr. Watts' words echoed like a scream through a hollow tunnel: "No reason is justifiable to teach hate. You can teach your child about love and accepting others all you want, but if there is no diversity in their toy box — and to this I would add to your circle of friends — you are a contributor to the racial tension in America." His words hung like a mirror, and I hid in fear from the woman and mother I had become. Just as I thought he was done, he went on: "We as parents must take a good look at our children's toy box. Loving others begins there."

His words found their way into me, untwisting my misconceptions and shaking the reasonable out of my justifications. In my earnest determination to offer my children a love of self and a sense of their own beauty, I had limited their toy box and their exposure to diverse dolls. That Christmas, my husband and I decided to gift our girls, now eight and six years old, with dolls. We drove to the store, sat for a long while in the parking lot, and then stood for an even longer time in the Dolls and Accessories aisle. I felt like a butterflied pig over a pit: roasting from a sense of betrayal to race, family, and self. Decisive people came and went while my children's father and I stood and stared up and down, side to side at an overwhelming number of white dolls, strategically placed at eye level, four or five Hispanic dolls beneath them, and two black dolls on the bottom shelf. Feeling a sense of rejection by the wider world, I was infuriated. The white dolls were accompanied by a change of clothes and a book. The Hispanic dolls and the black dolls had neither — but they were all listed at the same price. I was fighting to remain in the aisle, to muster the strength to purchase two dolls, when a repressed memory surged through me.

I was eight years old and I had whined to my grandmother for months about getting me a doll. When she finally purchased one, I was elated. It had blonde hair and blue eyes, and it was all mine. However, my grandmother had forgotten to tell me to keep it a secret from my grandfather. There is an actual picture of me holding it safely in my arms, but that was before my grandfather's eyes caught sight of me cradling what must have been in his eyes the spawn of Satan. He called me to his side, and I went with deference to the man I knew without a doubt loved me deeply. My grandfather's expression of love was not based on hugs or verbal affirmation, but instead, I knew my grandfather loved me dearly because of the rituals he created with me. An hour before the sun splashed orange and pinks across the island sky, we sat together beneath an almond tree in our front yard. I held his treasured Bible in my hand, read from Proverbs, and he closed his eyes to the sound of my voice. On Sundays, when my grandmother magically shared one chicken among twelve or more people, my grandfather saved his chicken bones with a little meat on each for me. He was a kind and soft-spoken man, dark as night with eyes the color of the sapphire. His hands usually reached out slowly toward me, but when I went to him this time, they came with a swiftness I had never seen. I could not calculate the speed with which he grabbed the doll from my arms and within seconds tore her to pieces. Parts of it went zooming past my head in various directions.

My grandfather was angry — maybe at my grandmother — but mostly, I later learned, for what the doll represented. My grandfather had been a farmworker. He had traveled to the United States to plant and harvest crops. Returning home each time his contract ended, he was a little more cautious of white faces. With each trip north he was beaten down with derogatory words, attitudes, and behaviors. Young white children, he once told us, chased his bus and threw rocks and sticks at the metal. He went on to say the children hurled the words black monkey at him and the other men inside. Sticks and stones barely made a dent in the bus, but words traveled through the glass and iron, hitting each man in the chest, striking each of them like poison darts.

My grandfather's dormant anger had turned into my dormant pain, and unconsciously I resorted to the no-toy-especially-white-dolls parental approach. As my grandfather had tossed pieces of my doll, he tossed the words at my grandmother, "Money is used for necessities, not foolishness!" I had come to associate purchasing a doll with squandering money. The phrase "squandering money" ejected me from that memory and put me back beside my husband in the Dolls and Accessories aisle. Purchasing a doll was going to be a difficult transition for me; purchasing a doll at such a price would be pure physical pain; purchasing a white doll was causing me major mental and psychological dissonance.

In the last throes of indecision I gave into my feelings. I was pissed. I was tossing questions and answers back and forth in my own head: why should I be the one to diversify my children's toy box? White parents should be doing this, not me. I remembered telling my friend a few weeks earlier about how black mothers had to be intentional when raising black children in America. "We have to supplement their education with books, we dress like it's Sunday for a simple doctor's appointment to ensure we appear worthy of the best care, and we constantly armor our children with words of affirmation." Then reason took over. My intent now, as hard as it seemed, was to raise children who were not prejudiced against people — white or otherwise.

I reached for a white doll and bent to pick up

a Hispanic doll. Robotically I placed them in my cart, stared at the dolls and their prices. I was getting ready to remove one of the boxes and put it back on the shelf when I thought about my girls. I thought about the friends they had made who resembled these dolls and I thought about how open their hearts already were. I thought about the new yearning I had, which was to be as open. I left both dolls in the cart. I took them home, where they joined the black doll already in my daughters' toy box.

Chapter Seventeen

COLOR

"Silence choked the space between us."

The first time I saw a white man I was seven years old. My cousins and I were playing bat and run in the front yard when we saw the man, hunched over and weighed down with some sort of contraption on his back. He had paused at the fork in the road just below us. There were two paths in front of him: the red dirt road to his right that would lead him to Mass Ferdie's house, and the rocky road that would lead him to our home atop the hill. He chose the rocky road, and as he mounted the hill, all seven of us — my siblings and cousins and me — searched each other's eyes then ran like fire in the direction of our outside kitchen, where Mama was cooking dinner.

The man might have chosen our house because of the scent of stew chicken — the marriage of onions, scallions, thyme, tomatoes, and fricasseed chicken — simmering over pimento wood. Mama tilted the lid of the dutchie to let some steam out. She listened to our tales so she could — as she would endearingly say — pick sense outta nonsense. That done, she walked ahead of us, wiping the stain of green bananas and yellow yam on the hem of her dress. We trailed behind her bravely, a tiny army of seven following our fearless leader.

Mama spoke to the man for a few minutes in the front yard, then invited him back into the kitchen. We followed behind them and sat on the makeshift bench, a long board held up by two cement blocks on either end. When the stew and its accompaniments were done cooking, Mama added an extra plate to the already long line of chipped enamel dishes on our table — an old door stacked on top of crates.

Ian, the white man, ate dinner with us that night. Due to scarcity, each member of our family had his or her own plate and cup. Ian ate dinner from his assigned plate and drank tea from his enamel cup for the month he was with us.

Uncle Dave, one of my mother's younger brothers, became Ian's pardy and companion, showing him all he needed to know — and not know — about being an honorary Jamaican. In the mornings, before the sun breathed in the dew drops of the night, Uncle Dave showed Ian how to tuck his pant legs into his water boots. He would also make sure Ian was leaving with a thermos of Mama's sweet cornmeal porridge. After a long day in the field, tending the yam mounds and sweet potatoes, Uncle Dave continued the task of teaching Ian. This time it was to fetch water in a bucket from the tank full of rainwater, find a corner, lather his rag with blue Carbolic soap, and wash the sweat of the day from his skin. Uncle Dave also tried to show Ian how to play ratta ratta on us children. However, Ian wasn't there long enough to learn how to steal flour dumplings from our plates.

When Ian left, we stood atop our hill and mournfully watched as he descended then mounted another hill leading up to Cumberland Church of God and faded out of sight. When I remember that time, I never once think about the color of our skins. Embedded in my psyche, however, is the dear memory of the warm camaraderie we all experienced in the month he was with us.

When I was ten years old, I migrated from Jamaica to the United States. Upon landing in Laguardia Airport, I became a black girl. I entered a new world, a slippery, twisted slope that began with my zip code: 07112. My parents lived in Newark, New Jersey, openly referred to as the black 'hood. It was one of the few places where immigrants trying to start a life could afford a home. My parents had bought a shell of a home for twenty-five thousand dollars. It had no plumbing or electricity. Before we arrived, my parents managed to live in it for a year while my father completely renovated it with his own hands.

The disparities between where we lived and where my parents worked were extreme. There were invisible fences created by our zip code — the five-digit number that determined the city, the school, and ultimately the education, or lack thereof, my siblings and I would receive. This angered my parents because my father risked deportation to make a better life for us. My parents bought into the mantra that America's education would be our saving grace.

My first entry into the educational system was a school severely lacking in resources. For two years I learned nothing new, nor was I challenged, because I already knew the information being taught. What the U.S. teachers were teaching in the sixth grade, I had already learned in the fourth grade in Jamaica.

After elementary school, I had two options for high school. One was a performance-based school where acceptance was rooted in one's artistic abilities. I tried singing. I was not accepted. The other high school was famous for gangs, drugs, joy rides, and shoot-outs. My Dad said, "Those two school options are shits." My parents were determined to find a new option. This would require a change of zip code.

My mother searched for a room to rent in Millburn — a white town that would change my zip code and allow me to attend Millburn High School. She located a room in the Sunday newspaper, phoned the landlady, and made an appointment to view the room. She was sure from their conversation the plan would be successful because the landlady, whose husband had died, was living alone and had said she would appreciate having company. My parents prepared me with the details. I would stay there for the week to attend school, and they would pick me up for the weekends.

My mother is a firm believer in three things: preparation, confirmation, and God. She called to confirm, and the landlady affirmed that she was awaiting our arrival. After forty minutes of driving, my mother pulled onto a street with neatly spaced houses on lush green lawns. My mother smiled at me warmly as we got out of the car. She held my hand, and we walked up the stairs admiring the flower pots on the covered porch. She rang the doorbell, and a gleeful white woman swung the door open. When she saw us standing there, her initial glow dimmed like an overloaded electric circuit. She retreated into herself like a turtle pulling its head under the protection of its hard

shell. She asked if she could help us. My mother proceeded to tell her who we were. The landlady grew angry. Her
words, "It's taken," pierced the air. She slammed the door
shut in our faces. The wealth of choice was not ours.

My mother's entire existence seemed to have frozen for a few moments, because it took a while before
I could feel the warmth re-enter her hand still holding
mine. She held my hand tighter as we walked to the car
in silence. I ached for my mother that day because, while
I heard her words of comfort and sensed the strength she
was trying to convey, I also sensed a stench of what I could
not yet name and a heaviness for which I had no words.
I had not known the intensity of my mother's pain, nor
did I know that a mother's heart could splinter into pieces
when her child is physically bruised, emotionally hurt, or
verbally injured. I would learn this agonizing heartbreak a
few years after becoming a mother.

No longer a little girl trailing behind Mama's
bravery or holding my Mother's hand, I grew into a wife

and mother myself. My family moved into The Village in Decatur, Georgia, so my husband could attend Columbia Theological Seminary. One of the great things about living in The Village was the neighbors; we looked forward to each change of semester announcing new families.

Sam, Sunny, and their three girls moved in five doors down from us. Our friendship was instantaneous. Although Sunny spoke very little English and stayed indoors often, Sam was an extrovert who enjoyed people, new ideas, and ways of being. He loved that I homeschooled, and together we made a pact: his two older girls would join our summer lessons from nine a.m. to noon, and he would teach my children the Korean language on Thursday afternoons at three. In the mornings, the girls kicked off their shoes at our doorway, ran upstairs to our school room, and once together with my children their learning began. We took lunch break at noon.

The children were like old sagacious friends. My sweet Korean neighbors and my brown babies seemed to

have learned the secret to idyllic summer days and en-
riched life in general. They sucked honeysuckles, played,
and lived every minute with childlike wonder. When the
children were together, they knew the magic, and the crux
of entertaining themselves.

While the children played, I became a fly on the
wall. I watched as they decided what to color in a new
Walt Disney coloring book, where none of the images re-
flected my sweet brown babies or our new Korean friends.
It was then that my little fellow — five years old at the
time — proposed they color a few characters brown. Livvy responded to Marko: "Brown is a poopy color."

Marko disagreed, "Brown is a pretty color," and off
they went, each defending his or her point of view. When
Sam returned, I explained to him the happenings of the
afternoon and how I had pointed out to the children that
brown is not poopy. He chortled awkwardly, and suggested that his little girl did not know anything about color.
Silence choked the space between us for the first time. I

searched for strength, quelled the anger and pain in my stomach, and retreated behind the walls and safety of our apartment. This experience was becoming too heavy.

It had been just a few weeks prior that during a playdate something else terrible had happened. My friend Gretchen called to tell me she would have to walk the kids down and talk to me. I expected everything but what she had to share. While the kids — her three white boys and my three melanated children — had been playing, her oldest told my middle child he no longer wanted to play with her brown skin. We sat on a log outside my door as the words forced their way through Gretchen's lips. They painted a picture of my daughter's face being drained of its sparkle as those assaulting words pierced her ears and tore through the feelings in her tiny chest.

As I listened, an aching rushed through me and uncontrollable tears fell onto my cheeks. Gretchen cried too. We looked at each other through red, swollen eyes. We hugged and cried, and she asked me sincerely, "How do I raise more conscientious, sensitive white boys?" It was a hard question, but it created a sacred space between us as we pondered it.

That evening, I washed the dirt from my children's hands and feet, then moisturized their cute faces, their sweet almond eyes looking up at me. I clothed them with words of affirmation using the tune of D'Angelo's song, "Brown Sugar Baby." The doorbell rang just after we had all found our way to the couch for me to read our nighttime story. Sam and Sunny were standing limply at our door, looking as though they had been through a storm. His face was lowered and her eyes were red with tears. Sam had obviously explained to Sunny what Livvy had said about brown being a poopy color. Sunny entered our home, sat on our couch, made space for my children beside her. With her limited English, she told each of them she was sorry.

Gretchen's question and Sunny's apology gave me some hope to know that they would be working on their end to expand their families' perception of what brown means to us. When our color is marginalized or erased, our history and struggle becomes invisible.

Chapter Eighteen

DETACHED

"I stuffed my confusion into a space I pretended for years never existed."

In my mind, I split my father in half around my sixteenth birthday. He was my dearly beloved Daddy. The relationship I had with him was brief; but the relationship I had with the man was buried deep in the grave of my belly. For years, I knew my father as the man who came to us from the clouds. Unlike my mother, who lived in the United States undocumented, my father's amnesty had allowed him the freedom to travel. Once a year around Christmastime he flew into Jamaica, where we lived with our grandparents. The festivities of Grandmarket Night, Jamaica's Christmas Eve party, matched my father's festive personality. Even before his arrival, preparations were made for him. The house and yard were cleaned, speciality meals were prepared, and we were washed sparkling clean and greased with Vaseline.

When my father arrived, he was like the red and green peppa lights that hung from trees. He brought with him new Christmas suits for my uncles and dresses for my aunties. He charmed the locals by taking trip loads of people out of Cumberland for the celebration. They squeezed in his small car, and he drove them there and returned to pick up another load. When we were all in Spalding Square, we could hear the sound of music escaping from each vehicle and plaza. The people laughed, chatted, and danced under the Jamaican twilight. My father bought rum for the men, Red Label wine for the women, and ice cream cake for the children. I was enamored and proud he was my daddy.

I was ten years old when I migrated from my grandparents' house to live with my parents in the United States. I was seventeen years old when my father died. In between those years, I learned that my father was a debonair individual. He entered the hearts of people through the doorway of a wink. In a room amassed with people, he would warm it, one wink at a time. How he learned this craft was beyond me. My father's weaknesses were Heineken, white rum, and women. His affairs had been discreet until one had lasted two years too long, breaking my mother apart one day at a time.

One night when he had consumed too much alcohol, he came home and joined the four of us — my mother, sister, brother, and me — on the pull-out couch. We had dressed it in sheets for family movie night. The movie ended and my mother, an early-to-bed kind of lady, said good night. My sister and brother hugged him good night and left for bed. I stayed. I lay on the sofa bed, and in moments, I no longer looked up to him. Instead, I found myself awash in pleasure, then shame. Our relationship was confusing to me afterwards, and I stuffed my confusion into a space I pretended for years never existed.

Daddy himself grew angry, and my punishments, mostly beatings, were extreme. One afternoon, I had a fashion show rehearsal in Orange, New Jersey, and Daddy was to drive me there. He told me to page him when I was ready to go and left for the bar. As Juliette, a young woman who lived in our basement, curled the last section of my hair, I paged him. But unlike other days when he showed up an hour later than scheduled, he came right away. I was not ready; a few strands of hair that would create a swoop across my forehead were left uncurled. His fury at my not being ready was as hot as the curling iron. He grabbed me by the lapel of my dress, yanked me from my chair, and threw me into the closet. When I turned to bury my face into my knees, my nose touched a six-inch iron stake that protruded from the wall.

With the unfolding of my thirties, the shame that had been deep inside slipped from its pit up into my consciousness. Twelve years after my father died, I awoke from a deep slumber, aware of how much I had buried. The bandages holding me together — put on one at a time over many years — began to unravel.

At thirty-two, I acknowledged that I had buried stillborn thoughts, unaddressed offenses, and shameful secrets. I had become physically and emotionally exhausted from being pretentious. I had grown accustomed to keeping an extremely clean and orderly house, putting dinner on the table at five, and pushing a stroller around our neighborhood after dinner. It was as if doing so would somehow make up for the secrets of my life. The secrets hidden beneath my wide smile and loud laughter were suffocating me in my self-made coffin. I felt there were no more places to tuck anything away, and I began to spill out like fat over skinny jeans. I ached in my chest, and I cried without words to clarify why. I was being summoned into a new space. I was afraid of letting go; I was afraid of moving ahead. It would be made clear that I had to in the most unlikely of places: in a moment of intimacy.

My husband looked me in the eyes and pierced me with a penetrating pause. His eyes, sweet like simple syrup, had turned on me with deep concern. They uncovered me, stripped away my pretense, sent me cowering in the corner like a child after the blow of a fist. I tried mustering up the strength to seem whole. He stared more intently and melted the hardness, the shield my secret had placed between us. He had caught me pretending and had the nerve to ask: "What is it that's holding you back from being present with me?"

For months, I relied on words of assurance and flirtatious smiles to cover my omission. His concern grew, and for weeks he expressed it only in gentle glances in the car, a question mark on his face while we bathed our children, and when we laid our heads on our pillows. We were resting on the couch one night after putting our babies to bed when he asked if I was ready to let him in. My insides contracted, my chest tightened, and I felt in need of breath. Shame clogged my pores and crawled like mud into my nose, stuffing it full.

My eyes closed themselves, fearing his expression as I spilled myself into the expanse of his outstretched heart. I began to tell him my guilt, the awful secrets that I was sure made me too dirty and unworthy to be loved by anyone. I was six or seven years old, I confessed, when the nebulous words fondle this appeared on my forehead, highly visible to self-seeking men. It was an older cousin at first who rubbed himself against my body until he shook with pleasure; a family friend who locked the car door and forced his metallic tongue through my sealed lips and terrorized my mouth; a school police officer who left a New Edition CD and red roses in my locker; a high school gym teacher; and the last was Daddy. Disclosing the last offender's name was like pulling my body through shards of glass. The taste of blood in my throat, my head low, my body weak from the strength it required to let his name leave me. Naturally the image my husband had of my dad was shattered.

For my husband, memories of my father were pure. He was the man who gave him sporting money and who bought him his first big-boy bicycle that operated with a brake on the handle. I had to make a choice between saving my father's image and digging myself out from beneath the shame and guilt. In choosing myself, I had felt the air make its way up, into my throat and over my tongue. I had smelled the pungent stench of death leave me as the words escaped my mouth. I fell to the ground, awash in tears. I finally had the strength that comes with being free. I was ready to push forward.

None of the fondlers had penetrated my body, but they penetrated my mind and confused my emotions. They had become one face muddled into the term men that filled me with fear and disgust. I struggled daily to trust, to not transfer their selfish transgressions onto well-intentioned gentlemen. That night of confession is now a prism confining the faces of those who offended me. My husband, on the night I cracked open and shattered, sat and held me while I fell apart. He stayed with me on the floor, wiping my face, his eyes full of tears mirroring mine. It was during this same conversation that I apologized for not being able to share or embrace his love fully. I confessed that I often questioned if he really loved me as a person or if it was my body he loved.

Chapter Nineteen

LET GO

*"The words lined up in the corridors
of my memory and waited for me to
open my mouth. When I did, they
crawled out one at a time, irritating
my mouth like sand spurs."*

The dichotomy may have started early. It was as if my parents ripped out my bladder and carried it with them when they left me and migrated to the United States. I suffered incontinence. I habitually wet the bed I shared with my cousin who had the same malady. My grandmother encouraged, threatened, and bribed us. I was powerless, I couldn't stop. Her last resort was checking us in the morning and beating the offender.

One night when I discovered the warmth of newly released moisture beneath me, I committed my first crime. In the silent darkness, I widened my eyes to see if my cousin was sleeping. I patted her underwear and when I felt it was dry, I switched underwear and rolled her onto my wet spot. Dry and sure of my fate, I slept. In the morning, I watched with an aching conscience as our grandmother pulled the belt back and slashed it across my cousin's skin for wetting the bed, again.

When our family of five was reunited in the United States in 1991, I regained control of my bladder and later watched as my mother unfolded in a series of less messy, but somewhat odd habits of her own. She exercised anywhere. She did not need the common apparatuses of sweatpants, sneakers, or a treadmill. Instead, she acknowledged the indisputable truth that her body had come fully equipped to entertain itself. At home, she stretched while she brushed her teeth. Holding a toothbrush in her right hand, she lifted and extended her left arm to the opposite shoulder blade, then repeated this move over and over again. When she gargled with the nasty brown mouthwash, she alternated arms, turning from side to side, as if dancing to "The Twist." Randomly throughout the day, she shook her legs like a dog after peeing on a tree.

She watched the Chuck Norris TV show faithfully, for one reason: the end. In the last five minutes, Norris would spring into a drawn-out beatdown of his enemy. The storyline had only served to stimulate droplets of adrenaline, filling my mother to capacity by the time the climactic music began. As though they were on a first-name basis — Lorna and Chuck — she jumped to her feet, placed her right foot in front, her left foot slightly off kilter for balance, and raised her fists up to chin level. She kicked and punched the air, dodged invisible jabs, slammed an unseen enemy to our hardwood floor, and fought to the bitter end to gain victory. As a child, I shook my head in disbelief. Now as a mother of three, I can see it is another of her habits — then embryonic — that has unfolded in time to reveal its wisdom.

A few weeks before she traveled, my mother secured a corner in her bedroom. When she would think about the upcoming trip, she would place clothes, shoes, and toiletries in the corner. The day before her departure, she sat on the floor in front of her stack, and not once did she get up in a panic to get anything. Everything she needed for that particular trip was there waiting for her: clothes to fold, toiletries to tuck into the cavity of her shoes, and her Chanel No. 5 perfume rolled into a pillowcase. She then put a bottle of Lysol atop, zipped her suitcase, and placed it at the door.

Her habit had its impact. Several years ago, my three children and I visited my sister and her family in New Jersey. A few days before our return, I secured a corner in my sister's house, and like my mother, we packed, zipped, and placed suitcases at the door. My brother-in-law coined my nickname, Sergeant Slaughter. I was not Sergeant Slaughter. I was Lorna's daughter.

I was a mother now and my mother was grand-mother. It was this new dynamic that changed our relationship. For years we had lived around the corner; however, when my family moved from Florida to Atlanta, vacation with Grandma became a new idea. With summer vacation quickly approaching, she would have them for two weeks. It was a time of excitement for my mother and the kids, but pure anxiety for me. I should already have secured a corner for little dresses, shorts, underwear, toiletries, Legos, and stuffed animals; but instead, there was an emotional pile already overflowing in the corner of my mind.

I withdrew from my mother, with whom I usually spoke daily. When I did speak to her, I was passive-aggressive: laying down the order and the rules of my children's stay with her. I was controlling and demanded that she herself stay with the children at all times — "No one babysits, not even Pops." I knew the latter would hurt. Pops was a gentle-spirited man my mother had married several years before. They had started dating a few months before I became pregnant with my first child, and when I gave birth, he was in the hospital with my family. He had been named Pops by my daughter when she joined in on the chatter of the world. He had given me no reason to mistrust him; we got along well. He fixed my cars, helped me move into my house, and actually walked me down the aisle when I got married.

On my wedding day, my white veil had been light, requiring only the strength of my future husband's thumb and index finger to reveal my smile. Revealing my inner veil involved tears and snot. Ontonio had lovingly challenged me — he sat with me, walked with me, and embraced me through a breakdown that became a break-through. I was now very aware, very sensitive to how children can be violated. My mother, however, was unaware of the depth of my lifelong or recent struggles and my resulting need to control people with whom my children spent time. That sensitivity showed in my unrelenting demands and jagged controlling efforts. It was not just Pops I didn't want near my babies, but all men. Unsuspecting though they were, they carried the taint of foul men before them.

My decision to unpack the emotional pile in the corner of my mind meant I had to make a choice — continue imprisoning myself or shatter my mother. I was conflicted. She was so present in my life. She worked hard and came home, fed us, and spent her down time with us. Unpacking and releasing the trauma from my mind felt like I would be taunting her with the words a mother dreads, "How could you not see?"

I was seven years old when I began piling offenses

into the corner of my mind. My own children were now in this age bracket. The upcoming trip to Grandma's challenged my own blind spots. I feared missing the details of my children's days. I was afraid there might be stories they would be ashamed or scared to tell me upon their return. The day I called my mother, the muscles in my tongue grew heavy, as if it were laden with a new layer of wet concrete. The words spazzed around my inner being and made me dizzy with dread. I sat on a chair, and the words lined up in the corridors of my memory and waited for me to open my mouth. When I did, they crawled out one at a time, irritating my mouth like sand spurs. I must have somehow failed grammatically or in volume, because my mother had not heard me the first time. Or maybe my words were still burning her ears like acid. The man she loved and mourned, the man who had fathered me was also the man who held me atop his body as my twelve-year-old body realized fleeting pleasure and longing shame.

Chapter Twenty

PAIN

*"I held my breath often but learned
quickly it was impossible to hold my
breath past the pain."*

I was thirty-two years old when I perceived a battle raging in my abdomen. The pain was so intense yet familiar that it took me back to my thirteenth year. After two weeks of unbearable pain, murky red spots had marked the lining of my unmentionables. The blood had been proof that my body was not conniving or deceiving me, but that I was in fact giving birth to death.

When I was in high school and the pain charged through my body and settled like bricks in my back and abdomen, I struggled to stand, to sit, to even move. I mustered up the strength from deep within me and boarded the number 44 bus to Newark, then the number 13 bus to Lyons Avenue, and arrived home on Aldine Street. My body rolled itself into a ball, and I stayed in bed for two days. Unlike my friends who used medication to abate the pain, my body seemed to laugh at such a simple act. I wondered if I was broken and if pain could kill.

At the age of thirty-two my menstrual cycle started occurring twice each month. I held my breath often but learned quickly it was impossible to hold my breath past the pain. Months turned into a year of feeling like a volcano was erupting in my uterus and hot lava was dripping into all parts of my belly. I went on a twisting, winding road to find the cause of what was attacking me from the inside. In the beginning, the doctors smiled and said I was in great shape and looked amazing. I tried believing them, but walked away each time feeling unheard. The first time I felt I was not making it all up came during an ultrasound. The technician made a sad face and said, "You have two angry ovaries in there." When the doctor gave me the result of the ultrasound, she made light of it. "We found a few cysts on your ovaries, but everyone gets them."

During multiple trips to the emergency room, doctors prodded, poked, and gave me pain medication. Once, I was misdiagnosed with an STD and was injected with an unnecessary and unhelpful antibiotic. During a visit to urgent care, the physician pressed my abdomen and recommended I urinate into a cup. He tested my urine and found nothing. He referred me to a gynecologist turned psychoanalyst who implied the pain — the one that made me cry myself to sleep at nights — could be psychosomatic. Another time, another doctor recommended I do yoga for what she said was pelvic floor congestion. One too many dullard doctors entered rooms, penetrated my vagina with cold tools, made notes and suggestions, and left me without hope.

One day while looking into the mirror, searching my eyes, and questioning my mind, my phone rang. My husband was calling. As part of completing his Clinical Pastoral Education, he had visited and prayed for a young woman groggy from surgery. She mentioned the symptoms that had prompted her surgery and he recognized them as mine. She suggested that I, like her, might be suffering from a chronic and silent disease: endometriosis. She told him to call me and tell me, "The pain is real; you are not crazy." I cried.

She wrote the name of her surgeon and an online

support group on a yellow sticky note. I started my search. I read over two hundred posts from women suffering from endometriosis. I binge-watched way too many videos on YouTube. Then, I called the doctor she had recommended at the Center of Endometriosis Care. I received a twenty-five-page medical application. Upon review of my medical history, Dr. S. called me personally to let me know that I might have adenomyosis, pelvic-floor dysfunction, and quite possibly, endometriosis.

I made an appointment, held my breath, and cried my way through a diabolical pelvic-floor exam. He confirmed the first two possibilities — adenomyosis and pelvic-floor dysfunction. Endometriosis could only be discovered through exploratory surgery. I scheduled my hysterectomy that day. Two months and ten thousand dollars later, I showed up at Northside Hospital with my supportive husband beside me and my thirty-three-year-old body running empty.

Fifteen months after I was disemboweled, there

was a concert of knives slashing through my insides. My abdomen and lower back felt like melting pots of angry currents electrocuting me with spasms that forced me to gasp out loud. I fought the pain by lying on a heating pad dialed to its zenith. I hugged two ice packs to my abdomen to cool the fireballs bursting and falling inside. I had not known that even after surgery, the pain could return. Mine had.

Chapter Twenty-one

RELIEF

"Morphine was medicinal grace."

Oxycodone was the narcotic prescribed to me after being disemboweled like a samurai turned traitor. My
uterus, appendix, fallopian tubes, and cervix were ripped
from their homes, cut off from their source, spilled out
into unknown hands, and placed in some dark room either to be taken for a study or simply tossed like garbage.
These organs had once been connected to nerves. Now my
nerves were screaming, spraying sparks of fire in all directions. It was unbearable, as though I was being torn apart
and my brain was aware of every fiery spark. I wondered if
oxycodone would be the balm needed to calm the wounds
in my brain and the raw nerves in my abdomen.

Surgery a year or so earlier had gone well. Anesthesia had been supreme. I had no horror stories of
waking up during the operation, feeling every pull and
tug, my mind fully aware of the current state but unable
to object. None of that. Waking up from the grogginess
of this surgery had not been bad either. I had awakened
slowly to a dim light, my husband's voice, and his wel-
come-back smile. His lips mouthed the words, "Hi babe,"

and his pure brown eyes lovingly inspected my face. My mind had awakened first; my body joined about twenty minutes later. As though the supply of blood had been turned off, I slowly felt life re-enter my legs. It crawled at first, as though awakening deflated veins. Suddenly the crawl turned into a mustang's gallop up my legs and into my abdomen. I screamed out in agony for the nurse. She came to my bedside and gently showed me the device I could press for medicine. I did not hear her say the button would dispense a magical potion of morphine, and in a matter of nanoseconds, it would drip into my IV. I pressed the button and found myself no longer being tortured, but resting in the cool of a mountain lake. Morphine was my medicinal grace.

The afternoon my surgeon cleared me to go home, I sat up in the bed, bent over to put on my boots, and passed out. Bending down was work, and it had cut off the blood circulation between my abdomen and my brain. I stayed a few hours for observation and was then sent home with a few directives: expect pain, be tender and patient with yourself, and take your pain meds. I was given a prescription for oxycodone. The hospital gave me two pillows for my ride home: one to ease the pain in my rectum, the other to hold against my abdomen for relief. Neither helped. I felt every bump, turn, and stop. When my husband carried me up the fifteen steps to our bedroom, I felt the rise and fall of every step. It took weeks before I made it back down those stairs by myself. During those three weeks I experienced a lifetime of discovery, decision, and a battle with a tiny white pill.

My first night home, I missed the power of pressing a button and having the magic medicine drip its wonderment into my veins. I opened the bottle of oxycodone. After the pop of a pill, it took about twenty minutes for my head to feel light and hazy — as if all was well with my brain, with my body, and with the world. It was ephemeral. While it did not ease the pain, it did do two things: it sent a message to my brain to chill on the heavy thoughts, and it made me less emotional about recovery. My thoughts had been filled with poetic genius, but my hands were too lethargic to jot them down. I was free falling. The world and everyone in it had seemed marvelous. Then I fell into a deep sleep. I awoke, however, to a heinous world. Anger roared up in me and everything that seemed light, airy, and poetic before my nap now seemed heavy, oppressive, and painful.

My oxycodone prescription had been written to last two weeks. I stretched it out for a month after surgery. The last pill stood alone in the bottle, calling to me as fear and pain swam around in my belly. I had been willing to endure the emotional side effects. I had not been ready to face a day without the security of at least one pill. I had left this one to linger. I endured the pain until the need for a pill was absolutely crucial. Bent over in pain one night and unable to move due to the incision in my abdomen, I took the last pill to calm the hellfire streaking through my body. The cycle played out again. For the last time. I enjoyed the short moment of mindful bliss, peaceful sleep, and my new summer romance nap. I awakened a couple of hours later with my feet firmly planted on the edge of addiction.

I was emotionally and physically drained, my body awash in sticky sweat, my heart sitting just beneath the surface of my skin, pumping at an uncomfortable speed. I twitched and shook like a leaf falling in a late autumn wind. I fought fear alone and in an attempt to prevent my heart's escape, I cupped my chest and curled my body into my husband's chest and the security of his arms. I made myself as small as possible, my legs up to my chin. I was paranoid, my thoughts growing rapidly and increasingly morbid. I imagined I was having a panic attack, or a heart attack, or even worse, that I was dying. Dark thoughts of despair hovered. I prayed silently and paced around in my head, trying to find affirming words from a distant past. When I could not offer my tortured mind any comfort, I began to ask myself, what could possibly calm me down? When the only answer reverberating in me was oxycodone, I jumped off the bed, grabbed my phone from the bedside, and darted toward the bathroom.

In the small bathroom, in the blue light of my phone, I googled symptoms of oxycodone withdrawal. There it was. I was going through withdrawal: I was the only actor in a scary movie, directed and produced by this little white pill. The withdrawal lasted a frightening eight days. The first two days were the worst. I was a bag of bones, loose and scrambled in a canvas bag. I prayed and pleaded. Shaky, clammy, and terrified, I wrapped myself in a blanket, almost like a straitjacket, and begged my husband to squeeze me tight. I took long showers numerous times a day. I shook involuntarily. I cried and talked to myself a lot. I drank a lot of hot toddies and water. I bit my nails and prayed for myself and for those trapped in the haunted, mirrored house of addiction. I prayed for people I had not nor will ever meet, but whose struggle I was understanding all too well.

Chapter Twenty-two

COLD EFFORT

"I pulled air in through my nose, un-robed, and passed the gown over to him."

After a full hysterectomy, my quest for endome-triosis-related pain relief took me down another winding road. First, I adhered to the surgeon's plan by scheduling an appointment with a pelvic-floor therapist. She was a kibitzer. I learned all about her husband, their children, their house, their pet. I learned that therapy with her was not about my pelvic-floor problems, it was all about her. I left and did not return. I called the surgeon's office and asked for a referral to another therapist. For the next six months, I met Mandy in her office overlooking the co-nundrum that is Midtown Atlanta.

Two days a week I sat on a baby's Boppy to re-lieve the pressure in my rectum while I drove forty-five minutes each way for pelvic-floor therapy. The therapy was expensive, intense, intrusive, and downright embar-rassing. Our sessions commenced with medical foreplay. I knew my role: take everything off from the waist down, lie face up on the exam table. Mandy dimmed the lights and made small conversation while she massaged the area above my ovaries. She made large and small circular motions, pressed in, then asked me to explain what I was feeling. When she was done, I raised my legs and placed both my feet into the stirrups of the exam bed, open for what was next. Slowly and gently she inserted a dilator to encourage my tender vaginal muscles to relax. "They were tightened," she said, "from years of carrying around an inflamed uterus."

Pelvic-floor therapy was awkward, but none more so than the manipulation of my rectum to release other muscles grown tense. To avoid the obvious awkwardness of her finger coaxing me to relax, my thoughts meandered during my visits. I wondered what she really studied in school, what her practicum entailed, what she discussed with her husband over dinner, what he said when she said, "Hey, honey, I relaxed a rectum today. Do you want meatballs for dinner?" She questioned me often, wanting to know if my pain level was easing, but nothing had changed. She grew discouraged but managed to seem professional even when she suggested I see a naturopathic doctor.

I immediately made an appointment with the naturopathic doctor she recommended, one even more costly at $500 a session. Every other Saturday for a few months, she examined my life and attempted to find the cause of my suffering. She demeaned the diagnosis of what she called westernized pathology. According to her, my hysterectomy was not necessary, leading me to think being gutted like a fish could have been avoided. This depressed me. However, as she asked questions about my upbringing, environment, and diet, it seemed she cared for me as a person and not just another patient. She prescribed natural medicine. At her direction, I drank green water — ten eight-ounce glasses of water with eight to ten drops of chlorophyll. I ate gluten-free foods. When I lost thirty of my one hundred forty-two pounds, it scared me, my husband, and my family. The unspoken fear was that I had cancer and it was sucking out the little body fat I had, leaving its calling card in my razor-sharp, sunken collarbones.

My mother suggested I tried cryotherapy. She not

only suggested it, she called the office, made the appointment, and prepaid for my first visit. My husband drove me to the office in Buckhead — central northeast Atlanta. The office was pure zen — white countertops, white sheer curtains, bamboo shoots, and orchids. Gentle raindrop music seemed to be coming from the alabaster walls. The space calmed my mind, but cryotherapy agitated my body. I didn't know cryotherapy uses an icebox, its temperature set at an unimaginable negative 300 degrees Fahrenheit. That is 332 degrees below the freezing point. For cryotherapy, I stood in an erect, cold coffin.

While there was no mental preparation for entering the icebox, there were some physical necessities. I took off all my clothes and put on a white gown along with a pair of warm Alaskan booties. After I stepped into the cryogenic chamber, the blond wonder, with an obvious gym membership, closed the door and requested my gown. I pulled air in through my nose, unrobed, and passed the gown over the door to him. He then asked if I was ready, and I nervously told him no. He smiled a Southern bless-your-heart smile.

It was cold, but a few seconds later I learned it would get colder. Liquid nitrogen, used to instantaneously freeze food, swirled around my feet. It seduced me with its white breath, distracting me as it slowly froze each part of my body. It started with my legs, crept its way up, attacking my pelvic muscles, my chest, then finally grabbing firmly onto my neck. My head was safe only because it hung over the opening at the top of the chamber. The piercing of negative temperature through my bare body, and the later shock to stimulate the return of blood circulation, was pure torture. Shrieking, whining sounds and parts of songs embedded in my psyche escaped my lips and gave me some comfort. My husband chuckled, giving the attendant permission to laugh at my absurdity. I told the blond tech I knew he would talk about the lady who made funny noises in the chamber, but that he should give me some credit in the story because I was, after all, Jamaican, not a member of some bobsled team. He laughed. I got dressed, and the woman at the front desk asked if I would like to make another appointment. "No! Once was already too much." For five minutes I felt no pain — cryotherapy might have worked. But it did not. With the heat of the day and the thawing of my body, the pain resumed.

Chapter Twenty-three

NAMASTE

"My muscles burned beneath my skin, and I could not foresee mustering the strength to go beyond the quivering of my knees."

Heat and spice are among the words often used to describe my country of birth. I am familiar with the ripened sun producing tingles in the well of my pores. Meals spiced with Scotch bonnet peppers heat up the cavities of my intestines and produce a loud numbing sound in my ear. I am familiar with and welcome both heat and spice in life, but the heat and spiciness of Bikram Yoga was foreign, unfamiliar, and uncomfortable to me.

Bikram Yoga, plainly put, means hot yoga. The thermostat is set at 105 degrees Fahrenheit, the windows are closed, and no air enters or escapes the large meeting room. Its approach was subtle at first. In the heart of Decatur, Georgia, my husband and I sat on bamboo lounge chairs — fit for a Miami beachfront hotel or some island shoreline. We watched as seasoned students tossed greetings back and forth, and a feather-like instructor signed people in at the front desk.

When the instructor inquired if we wanted to sign up for a one-month trial at a discounted offer, I looked

her over and thought, I could take her in a tussle any day
— this is only yoga after all — bring it. My husband and I
signed up for the ninety-minute classes in the one-month
trial package. We could, for an entire month, come and
go as much as our little hearts and bodies could take. We
paid the price and walked away from each other into our
separate gender-labeled fitting rooms.

My changing room was not as cool as the front
entrance. It was set a few degrees higher, maybe to gradually woo us into the kind of heat that would soon challenge our breathing. The changing room itself displayed
a wonderment of women. The barriers of clothing were
off. The brown of my skin kept my shock and awe hidden. Depending on one's vantage point, there was a
room full of half dressed, half naked, or completely naked women taking showers in stalls without glass doors
or curtains. Women from all age groups were represented. They were moving about with grace; modeling perky
or sagging breasts of all cup sizes; displaying thick, lean,
and in-between thighs; revealing clean-shaven and hairy

fronts; as well as firm, plumped, and otherwise back ends. I was clearly overdressed in my mid-thigh tights and airy aqua-blue activewear top. I was carrying the wrong mat. I would soon learn the fewer clothes the better — a thong and headband would have sufficed. My Pilates mat was a centimeter or two too thick.

The fitting room opened to a brief and narrow walkway. It was a small breathing space for the final inhale of cool air to last the next ninety minutes. A heavy-duty curtain brushed the floor just ahead, and when I reached my hand out to shift the curtain out of the way, it was as though the mouth of a furnace had opened. There was a marriage of heat from the 105-degree room, muddled with the spice of varying body odors, and the addition of new perfume mixed with old sweat. These scents seeped into the dingy brown and green carpet and funneled into the orifices of my body. Heat and spice slithered up my nostrils and I swatted my nose as if a fly had tickled the inside.

I entered the room, found my space beside my husband, and adjusted my breathing in the merciless heat. I made small talk with those around me, then watched as the instructor eased in almost as though she was floating on the backside of a crisp fall day. She glided to the front of the room, and the class stood in synchrony, like a communal song of movement. I followed them — out of tune and a little off-key.

The instructor's voice was soft. She guided us into childlike movements until she told us to keep the pose for the count. Those words were said with such ease, but as we stood like images frozen in time, she counted like a child who stuttered. "Keep the pose for the count," she repeated — and mockingly whispered, "Soon you will meet your maker." With each pose, I felt an organic need to do one of two things: shake my body like a dancing toddler or channel my inner Deepak Chopra, speaking words of encouragement to my mind and muscles. Without ceasing, the instructor guided us right into the next stance, as though burning was the prerequisite for the upcoming pose. There was a gradual build of heat pumping through my arms and legs, pushing like weights against my best intentions. My inhales and exhales grew confused, and the sounds I usually quelled, the ones indistinguishable between pleasure and pain, escaped me. I wondered why I was doing yoga at all. What was the point of this self-inflicted pain? I suddenly felt about Bikram Yoga the way I feel about roller coasters and scary movies. Who the hell pays to intentionally torture themselves?

The heat produced by the movement of seized-up muscles was intense and my response was borderline embarrassing and holy. I whimpered, which is a sort of prayer, in the meditation room inside my mind. The pros, the mini-Buddhas in the room, balanced themselves on their hands, raised their buns in the air, stretched their legs out, and raised their heads towards the ceiling. They reached the zenith of peace, all while I struggled not to faint. I had fought for far too long, and then I hissed through my teeth and began my walk of shame towards the door. Miss Fragile Instructor was attentive. She caught me like a frog would catch a fly on the tip of its tongue and pulled me back in with her calm, encouraging words: "The dizziness will pass. Just sit and regroup." I was both a little irritated for being called out and relieved that it had happened to others. I sat on my Pilates mat, and watched while each well-aligned, zen-like mini-Buddha held the pose and flashed me encouraging smiles.

I thought I had recovered a few minutes later. I gathered my thoughts and body, and I stood on my feet. The instructor — whom I could obviously not take down in a tussle any day — smiled wisely at me. She continued to instruct the class: twist your arms like a pretzel, cross your right leg over your left thigh, bend your knees and stoop down as if you're going to have a seat. She counted slowly. My muscles burned beneath my skin, and I could not foresee mustering the strength to go beyond the quivering of my knees. Just as the words "I have no more in me" surfaced and I began to believe them, the instructor softly said, "I know you're tired... but you're almost there....We're almost at the end."

Trusting her words and a newfound confidence forming within myself, I pushed through, but not without making the sounds of a gorilla in heat. The class colleagues held their poses, but when we were instructed to lie down for the last stretch, they all laughed — maybe because I had verbalized something we were all feeling. My knees had buckled and I had crumpled to the floor, flapping my legs about briefly like a Japanese mudskipper. I had lain on my Pilates mat and looked up at the ceiling, which then led my eyes toward the white and blues of the sky. My entire being had awakened — I felt every muscle in my body throb, blood run through my veins, and my heart pump a bubbly hello! With each ninety-minute class for the next month, I unfolded and greeted dormant muscles, resulting in the freeing of my mind. Hello, Muscles. Hello, Breath. Hello, Mind. Namaste.

Chapter Twenty-four

BLUE PAINT

"I tried. I griped. I cleaned. I sprayed.
I escaped outside."

The Big Ol' House with all its contradictions was a prayer answered. My husband was two weeks away from graduating from seminary and we still had not found a home for when we would move off campus. When a friend called to tell me a For Rent sign had just been posted in the yard next door to her sweet family, it was our only open door. I called, made appointments, submitted paperwork, and we signed a one-year lease just a few days before we had to move. Family members flew in from California, Jamaica, and Florida to celebrate my husband's graduation and help me pack so we could move into the Big Ol' House.

Our new home on Cloudland Drive was designed and built by an artist in 1962. It had housed decades of comings and goings: memories embedded in the wooden floors, laughter and tears soaked into the walls, and scents of the past mingled and lingered in the air. It was a ranch-style home with a bipolar personality. My response to it was split between perplexed and intrigued. The exterior walls were made by local artisans who engraved their initials into each red brick. The entrance was grand. There were two oversized black doors that opened to the entry hall. The interior brick wall, robbed of its earthly red, was painted black. It required me to pause and ponder my next step: to the left or to the right?

The entire left side of the house was dark. It hosted the three bedrooms and two bathrooms, all of them trapped in the '60s with no way to escape through the small windows. The walls, once white, were dressed in dingy white, with a tint of brown from years of assault by dirty hands. Dust adhered to the blinds in the bedrooms, and the mirrored closet doors were trimmed in gold. The bathroom did not escape the interspersing of gold on the fixtures and the knobs on chipped brown cabinet doors. The cabinets and drawers were mildewed and gave off a scent of rot. There was a tissue box holder, a hip design in its time, that was cut into the bathroom walls. One bathroom wall was covered in blue tiles, and the other in yellow — each of them missing a few tiles like children missing their baby teeth.

Opposite of the left side, the right side was immaculate. It was an artist's dream where the walls were made of glass. The first room was long and narrow, with the stretch of two white walls, vaulted ceiling, and mahogany wood floor. This room became a perfect host for our treasured books and my husband's original, colorful paintings.

A step up led to the formal dining area, where the sun's light danced on the dark floor. To the left was the kitchen and beyond that was the living room, with a late add-on that stretched out and over the backyard like a massive glass treehouse jutting out into the arms of a forest. In this space, there was nowhere to hang pictures or paintings; instead, the trees and flowers outside filled the eyes with nature's art. A wraparound deck, appropriate for parties, overlooked a lower level of the backyard. An expansive rose bush bloomed, and pink flowers fell to the ground like a gown to the feet of a bride. The scent of gardenias whiffed from the neighbors' yards, and the songs of unseen birds sung from high trees. The light and beautiful right side of the house inspired elaborate gestures. Months after moving in, on our tenth wedding anniversary, I adorned myself in my wedding dress — veil and all. My husband donned his suit and the kids dressed in their Sunday best. Our six-year-old son officiated a private service in our backyard. We renewed our wedding vows and danced barefoot for hours on the art and book room's mahogany floor.

My own village — which is to say, hardworking, opinionated family members and sweet friends — joined hearts, heads, and hands to help us move in and make our new house habitable. People showed up in varying ways and offered whatever skills they possessed. My hand-sanitizing, germaphobe sister-in-law attacked the kitchen cabinets with bleach wipes and the vengeance of a scientist. My mother, who has magic hands for laundry, separated, washed, and dried loads of clothes, towels, and sheets. She did not fold with the same enthusiasm. My mother-in-law, however, folded each piece with reverence and placed them on shelves as though they would never be used again. Our neighbor Josh brought his toolbox and his children. He tediously measured and hung each curtain rod. He asked for the placement of our family photos, then hammered hooks into the wall, and hung our pictures with care. Tiny hands inserted room fresheners into almost every unoccupied outlet.

I sought to conform the interiors of the Big Ol' House — making the left side match the right — but it was of no use. The house continued to be its split self. I could not mask the mildew scent that the kitchen sink burped up and out into the air. The tricks of using hot water, essential oil, lemon peels, and ice in the garbage disposal were of no use. The room fresheners and scented candles suffocated under the stifling old smells. I tried. I griped. I cleaned. I sprayed. I escaped outside.

It was the exterior that fed me. Without fail, it invited me into a meditative space and opened my eyes to see for the first time fuchsia flowers with a personality. In the cool of the morning, my husband and I drank our coffee while sitting on two rocking chairs I had salvaged from the roadside. The flowers opened themselves up as if to breathe in the glory of the morning. Around ten, when the sun pronounced it day, the flowers closed their petals like weary eyes and went to sleep until twilight. They did not ride the well-known progression of the day, but instead slept while people busied themselves. I wondered if they felt lazy. Then I wondered if I was insane for placing emotions on flowers. But their exquisite existence and the peace all around encouraged my pondering, and I could not help but reflect.

During our time in the disjointed house, I became awake, aware of my dualities, and the direction of my growth as a person. I had gone against the norm in so many areas of my life, and I now wondered if I was just exhausted from the energy it required to keep afloat. Like flowers, I was blossoming. I might not open in the sunlight, in the heat of the day; and I might not open when expected, but I was opening during my own peak hours.

As I painted the two rocking chairs blue, I remembered my father in his brokenness. The pain he had caused me, my emotional breakdown as a result, and my negative views towards men and sex. Tears streamed from my eyes, mixing with the paint, and I found the release I had been seeking for too long. With each stroke of the brush, his voice that I had pushed to the far reaches of my mind re-emerged. The volume had been turned back on, and I heard my father's voice guiding me as he did the summer he taught me to paint. The art of painting, without leaving streaks, is in the wrist and following it all the way up and down. Do not break the stroke on your own. I remembered his winks and how they warmed the girl within me. I now understood that he came from brokenness and tried his best to escape. The blue paint was transforming the old chairs. The balloon of pain that I had carried against my father burst, fell onto my face, and into the blue paint, transforming me.

Chapter Twenty-five

COMING HOME

*"Hurting and healing abound in the
mess of it all."*

My middle baby and I went on a mini date to the library. At the library, she returned a Judy Moody book then picked out a new one while I searched the sales rack for a book to call my own. When I spotted Year of Yes by Shonda Rhimes, I bolted towards it, internally pledging to outrun anyone who dared to come close to it. I purchased it for one dollar. It was mine. I was free to underline words or sentences and write my own thoughts in the margins. We left the library pleased with ourselves. I felt light with only one child, so I reached for my daughter's hand and she happily took mine as we walked airily to our car. Life was easy with one. I glanced at her as we split — her to the passenger side and me to the driver's — and suddenly marveled at the miracle of transformation. I had once held her as a little baby, cupping her head and tiny buttocks to lay her in a car seat. I had lifted her as a toddler and buckled her into the booster. Now I watched as my nine-year-old girl opened and closed her own door, adjusted in the seat, and fastened her own seat belt, then gazed out the window, awash in her own thoughts. On our drive home, we stopped for yogurt.

We sampled over ten flavors. We compared them to the flavors that pleased our palates during a culinary adventure at the Yogurt Tap in Georgia. Comparison is like feeding yourself poison in a champagne flute. We finally decided to be present and purchased two yogurts. Zahara walked ahead of me and chose a table outside in front of the pink crape myrtle flowers, with an umbrella overhead shielding us from the sun. We ate. She talked. I listened intently to this little girl because she struggles with articulating certain letters and sounds. Most days, as her mother and teacher, I am steadfast in reminding her to slow down, but not today. Today, I pulled closer and listened deeper. I listened earnestly because she is an old sage — an old soul inhabiting a nine-year-old body.

"If I could build a perfect city," she said, "I would have the beaches from southwest Florida, the Yogurt Tap from Georgia, and Gunther's Ice Cream in California." Her perfect city would have all her favorite things and people, each inspired and gathered from places we lived in her short nine years.

I thought about the places I too had lived, gathering up experiences and moments in my mind. I had arrived at each address apprehensive, but had found meat and meaning with all that transpired. I always left bruised a little, enlightened a lot. Transformed. Each place had been like school — filled with people posing new challenges, provoking internal conflicts, and demanding I look inward, shift, or remain stuck in my Me-ness. I came to understand that thoughts, understandings, and perspectives left unchallenged or unchanged are like wading in murky, stagnant waters. I explored and let go of ideas that no longer sustained me. I found myself sitting there eating yogurt, grateful for growth.

At the same time, I found myself grateful for the stories and insights I held onto, those passed on to me from my parents. I know for certain that my Dad was right, "Life is hard as shit, and people are as kind as they are assholes." Life beats up on you at every turn. It leaves marks, some barely touching the skin, while others are excruciating and deep, leaving us wounded, scarred, and scared.

I've made peace with my father being broken and beautiful. I can still feel his presence in the rattle of a key, and though faint, I can still hear his voice defending me. I've made peace with my mother. There are no more secrets between us. Her sacrifices have made my life possible. In my memory, I can hear the machete hitting Daddy's flesh and at the same time I can see Daddy and Mommy standing beneath the light at the front door. I can hear him whisper, "Cum mek mi whispa someting sweet inna yu ears." I don't know what they shared, but whatever the words were, Mommy nestled into his neck and laughed heartily.

There is power in the insights I have gained. What I've come to adopt as new truth, and how we choose to live in the face of that universal truth, is permeated by two extremes. The dirty trick is having to discover on one's own that these two extremes are not far apart. Hurting and healing abound in the mess of it all.

Truth is real. It settles deep within, measures, and

guides me. I revel in the stability of my hard-earned understanding. But I also find myself often just meandering through the joy that has embraced me at every turn — simple yet significant. I have learned to love the flow of life. I have learned not to fret. I have learned to welcome and embrace, and say goodbye. I have learned to make home wherever I go. I have learned that, even in this moment, I AM home.